THE RIDDLE DECODED:

NIK KERSHAW AND THE ART OF PERFECT POP

UNOFFICIAL AND UNAUTHORISED

LAURA SHENTON

THE RIDDLE DECODED:
NIK KERSHAW AND THE ART OF PERFECT POP

UNOFFICIAL AND UNAUTHORISED

LAURA SHENTON

IRIDESCENT TOAD PUBLISHING

Iridescent Toad Publishing.

©Laura Shenton 2025
All rights reserved.

Laura Shenton asserts the moral right to be identified as the author of this work.

No part of this publication may be reproduced, stored or transmitted in any form or by any means, electronic, mechanical, photocopying, recording, scanning, or otherwise without written permission from the publisher. It is illegal to copy this book, post it to a website, or distribute it by any other means without permission.

Designations used by companies to distinguish their products are often claimed as trademarks. All brand names and product names used in this book and on its cover are trade names, service marks, trademarks and registered trademarks of their respective owners. The publishers and the book are not associated with any product or vendor mentioned in this book. None of the companies referenced within the book have endorsed the book.

All cover images used under a commercial licence.

First edition. ISBN 978-1-917969-12-3

Contents

Preface: A View from the Outside	11
The Sound of the Machine: 1984 and the Pop Industry's Perfect Storm	15
The Art of the Deal: How to Sell a Ready-Made Star	19
Before the Solo Flight: The Fusion Foundation	23
Third Time Lucky: The Resurrection of a Nuclear Pop Classic	29
Critical Misfires: When the Press Got It Wrong	33
A Nice Surprise from Across the Pond	37
The Price of the Ride: Learning to Be Famous in Real Time	41
The Quintessential Eighties Icon: From Unemployment Benefit Office to Pop Stardom	47

The Comparison That Wouldn't Quit: Nik Kershaw, Howard Jones, and Journalistic Shorthand	51
Surprising Influences in Rock	55
The Riddle of The Riddle: When Commerce and Creativity Collide	59
Music First, Words to Follow	63
A (Slightly) Warmer Reception from the Critics	65
Vision and Video: The Visual Language of Kershaw's Success	69
The Weight of Wembley: Kershaw at Live Aid	75
Live at The Ritz: Kershaw Commands New York	79
Under the Bonnet: The Musical Architecture of Kershaw's Songs	83
Dancing Girls	86
Wouldn't It Be Good	89
Drum Talk	92
Bogart	94
Gone to Pieces	96
Shame on You	99
Cloak and Dagger	102
Faces	105
I Won't Let the Sun Go Down on Me	109
Human Racing	112

Don Quixote	114
Know How	117
You Might	120
Wild Horses	122
Easy	126
The Riddle	128
City of Angels	132
Roses	135
Wide Boy	138
Save the Whale	141
Beyond the Breakthrough Period: The Later Eighties Albums	145
The Long Game: Beyond 1984 and Back Again	151
Finale: The Enduring Magic	155

Preface: A View from the Outside

There's a particular kind of magic that happens when you truly listen to a Nik Kershaw song. It might catch you on first hearing – that infectious melody, that unexpected chord change – or it might reveal itself years later, when you suddenly notice a bass line weaving through the mix that transforms everything you thought you knew about the track. For over forty years now, listeners have been discovering and rediscovering these moments, finding new depths in songs they thought they knew by heart.

It's this ongoing conversation between artist and audience that brings us here. This book is a celebration, not a biography. The story of Nik Kershaw's life belongs to him alone, and perhaps one day he'll choose to tell it in full. What these pages offer instead is something different: an exploration of Kershaw as songwriter and craftsman, viewed through the lens of music appreciation.

At the time of writing in late 2025, Kershaw himself is touring venues across the country, sharing his own stories about these songs – the official word, straight from the source. His insights into his creative intentions represent the definitive account and should always be regarded as such. This book makes no attempt to second-guess what was in his mind when he wrote his songs. That territory is his alone.

What we can claim, however, is our own experience as listeners. From the moment 'Wouldn't It Be Good' first crackled across radio waves to the countless times we've returned to these songs across four decades, we've formed our own relationship with this music. This book examines that relationship – what we hear in the grooves, what patterns emerge in the harmonies, what makes certain lyrical turns stop us in our tracks. It's the view from the outside looking in, where millions of us have stood, watching one of British pop's most distinctive talents at work.

The journey begins in 1984, that remarkable year when Kershaw seemed to arrive fully formed into a musical landscape dominated by synthesizers and shoulder pads. To understand the magnitude of what he achieved, we need to examine that moment in time – the industry he entered, the competition he faced, and the unique space he carved out for himself. From there, we'll undertake a detailed exploration of every track from *Human Racing* and *The Riddle*, the two albums that established his reputation and contain the DNA of everything that would follow. Selected highlights from his later work will round out our discussion, but the focus remains firmly on those formative years when a young man from Suffolk revolutionised what British pop could be.

I write this as an outsider – unaffiliated with Kershaw or his associates, armed only with a musician's ear, an academic's analytical tools, and a fan's deep appreciation. This is an unofficial tribute from someone who, like many of you, has spent years marvelling at how Kershaw could make complexity sound effortless, how he could hide sophisticated harmonies inside perfect pop songs, and how he could write lyrics that revealed new meanings with each listen.

The magic of Nik Kershaw's songwriting doesn't need my validation, or anyone else's. It speaks for itself every time someone discovers that 'The Riddle' isn't actually a riddle, or hears the political commentary in 'I Won't Let the Sun Go Down on Me,' or finds themselves humming a bass line that's far more intricate than they'd ever noticed. But sometimes it's worth pausing to examine why something works, to appreciate the craft behind the catchiness, and to celebrate an artist who never took the easy route when a more interesting path was available.

This book is that pause – a chance to look closely at songs we thought we knew, and to discover that we're still only scratching the surface.

The Sound of the Machine:
1984 and the Pop Industry's Perfect Storm

By 1984, the pop music industry had evolved into a finely-tuned mechanism, three decades removed from the wild frontier days of rock and roll's birth in the 1950s. Through the laboratory of the sixties and seventies – with their concept albums, stadium tours, disco booms and punk explosions – the business had learned its lessons well. Record labels now understood the mathematics of hit-making: how much to invest in production, how many singles to release, which radio stations to court, what image to craft. The machinery of stardom had been stress-tested by everyone from The Beatles to Bowie to Motown, and by 1984, executives knew precisely which levers to pull.

Into this well-oiled system stepped Nik Kershaw, arriving at a peculiar moment of transition. He landed just ahead of the next evolution in pop manufacturing – the Stock, Aitken and Waterman hit factory that would soon reduce pop success to an almost algorithmic certainty. Where SAW would perfect the art of the three-minute assembly line, Kershaw still belonged to an era where songwriters could smuggle jazz chords and complex arrangements into the charts under the cover of a catchy chorus.

Sonically, Kershaw's first two albums are unmistakably children of their time, swimming in the crystalline keyboards, synthesizers, vocal and percussion effects that practically define 1984. Some might dismiss this sound as dated – that particularly eighties combination of synthetic drums and glossy production that can make everything sound like it was recorded in the same studio, on the same day, by the same programmer. But to focus on the era's sonic uniform is to miss the extraordinary tailoring happening underneath. In more recent years through online interviews featured on YouTube, Kershaw himself has reflected on the fate of those period instruments – how items that were once seen as essential parts of the studio toolkit ended up in skips when fashion moved on, too expensive to maintain and too "eighties" to be cool.

Yet here's the fascinating paradox: in 1984, this wasn't a tired sound but a thrilling new frontier. When *Human Racing* hit the shelves in February, the synth-pop revolution was still actively revolving. A-ha's 'Take On Me' – now synonymous with eighties pop perfection – wouldn't conquer the charts in its familiar form until the following year. The Pet Shop Boys hadn't even released their first single. Kershaw wasn't following a template; he was helping to write it.

Whether a modern listener embraces or endures that quintessentially eighties production likely determines their relationship with Kershaw's catalogue today. It's telling that his recent YouTube uploads of stripped-down, acoustic performances reveal songs that transcend their original packaging – proof that beneath the period dress lies timeless songcraft. Yet to dismiss the original productions would be to lose something essential. That eighties sheen isn't mere nostalgia; it's integral to the music's DNA.

This is the beautiful contradiction of Kershaw's early work: songs sophisticated enough to work in any arrangement, presented in production that could only have existed in that specific moment. The sound might carbon-date the recordings to 1983-84, but like all the best period pieces, they're more powerful because of their specificity, not in spite of it. They're vital features, essential elements of a sonic time capsule that captured lightning in a very particularly-shaped bottle.

The Art of the Deal:
How to Sell a Ready-Made Star

In the mythology of pop stardom, we often imagine talent being "discovered" – the A&R scout in the dingy club, the demo tape that lands on the right desk by cosmic accident. But Nik Kershaw's entry into the music business reveals something far more calculated and clever: an artist who understood that talent without strategy is just expensive hobby equipment gathering dust.

The evidence lies in a few column inches of classified advertising that appeared in *Melody Maker*: "MANAGEMENT URGENTLY REQUIRED FOR YOUNG MULTI-TALENTED ARTIST. Top record company interest. I've done all the work, all you have to do is sell me. Send name and address for complete package (tape, photos, video, etc.)."

Every word of this advert reveals strategic thinking. The urgency creates momentum. The claim of "top record company interest" establishes pre-selection value – even if that interest was tentative or exploratory, it signals this isn't a bedroom dreamer but someone already in the conversation. But the masterstroke is that middle sentence: "I've done all the work, all you have to do is sell me." Kershaw positioned himself not as raw potential requiring development, but as a finished product requiring only distribution.

Mickey Modern, who would answer that call and become Kershaw's manager, recognised the advert's unusual ambition. As he recalled in a 1984 television interview, "It was quite a big advert, really. All the others were really small. I thought I might as well answer it because I've had dozens of tapes. Two weeks later, the tape came and this young man called Nik Kershaw. I put it on and it was immediate. Fantastic. It was most of the first album, actually."

That last detail is crucial – "most of the first album." Kershaw wasn't sending out half-formed ideas. He was shipping a complete artistic statement, ready for the next step of the journey. Here was someone who had done the groundwork and had the material to prove it. This was the equivalent of a tech startup approaching venture capitalists with a working product and existing customers rather than just a PowerPoint presentation. Modern didn't need to imagine what Kershaw might become; he could hear exactly what he was. The partnership clicked, and it was Modern who would broker the deal with MCA Records that would launch everything that followed.

Yet Kershaw himself has never presented this success as inevitable. In numerous interviews over recent years, he's been refreshingly candid about the role of chance in his breakthrough. His work was turned down plenty of times, he's admitted, and he remains acutely aware of how many other musicians were striving for the exact same opportunity. He has reflected on all the other talents out there, whose work simply never found its moment in the spotlight. (As he wrote for the dedication page in his 2001 book, *Spilling the Beans on Making It in Music*, "For all those beautiful, talented people who didn't get lucky.")

It's a sobering thought – how many *Human Racing*-calibre albums never made it past the demo stage? How many potential classics are sitting in attics, victims not of lacking talent but of lacking timing, connections, or simply the forward-thinking to take out a sizeable advert in *Melody Maker*? The music industry of the early to mid-eighties, for all its evolved machinery, still had a brutally narrow gateway. For everyone lucky enough to squeeze through, it's plausible that dozens of equally gifted artists were left standing outside.

This makes Kershaw's breakthrough both a testament to his business acumen and a reminder of music history's sliding doors moments. His strategic thinking – understanding that he needed to present himself as an investment opportunity rather than an artistic project – was as crucial as his ability to craft a perfect pop song. But even he acknowledges the element of fortune in Mickey Modern actually playing that tape, actually hearing what was there, actually having the connections to make something happen, and indeed, MCA giving them that all-important 'yes.'

We're left with a curious duality: celebrating Kershaw's savvy in engineering his own breakthrough while contemplating the phantom discography of all those who weren't quite savvy enough, connected enough, or simply lucky enough. That we get to enjoy 'Wouldn't It Be Good' and 'Dancing Girls' isn't just because Kershaw could write and record brilliant pop songs. It's because he also understood that in the music business, being good isn't good enough – you also need to be smart, prepared, and just a little bit fortunate.

Before the Solo Flight: The Fusion Foundation

To understand Nik Kershaw's seemingly sudden emergence in 1984, we need to rewind to 1980 and a band called Fusion, whose sole album *Till I Hear from You* provides crucial context for what was to come. This wasn't some garage band demo – it was a sophisticated, diverse effort that reveals Kershaw as part of a genuine musical collective rather than a solo artist waiting to break free.

The most striking discovery is 'Look Behind You,' which would eventually metamorphose into 'Human Racing.' The melody is identical – note for note what would become a hit four years later. The arrangement differs, but here's proof that some of Kershaw's most successful ideas had been percolating long before MCA took him under their wing. It's a fascinating glimpse into the creative process, showing how great melodies can wait patiently for their moment.

What's immediately apparent listening to Fusion is that this was emphatically not 'Nik Kershaw and some backing musicians.' The album bristles with collective energy – complex arrangements featuring brass-style sections, funk rhythms, jazz progressions, and rock dynamics. Tracks like 'Till I Hear from You,' 'Play Around,' and 'Big Brother' could have come from Ian Dury and The Blockheads' catalogue, sharing that same intelligent pub-rock sensibility that was still currency in 1980. This is sophisticated music that somehow remains accessible, never disappearing up its own experimental backside.

'Play Around' is rocky and punky in that distinctly early-eighties way; it showcases Kershaw's vocals adapting perfectly to a completely different musical context than his later pop work. The track's unexpected rhythm changes and diverse sections – this isn't verse-chorus-verse predictability – demonstrate real musical ambition. In some alternate timeline where synth-pop never happened, you can imagine Kershaw fronting a critically acclaimed post-punk outfit, his voice just as comfortable over angular guitars as it would later be over synthesizer presets.

The extended instrumental sections throughout the album tell their own story. Kershaw wasn't the frontman here, wasn't even necessarily the leader. Those long breaks where the instruments take over – sometimes for minutes at a time – speak to a democratic approach where everyone got their moment. This was a proper band, likely with all the creative tensions and collaborative magic that implies.

The album's back cover reinforces this democratic spirit. All four band members are featured equally, each occupying their own quarter with a black and white portrait alongside their credits: Reg Webb – keyboards and vocals, Kenn Elson – bass and ACME thunder, Alan

Clarke – drums, Nick Kershaw – guitar and vocals. Note the spelling: this was still 'Nick' with a 'c,' before the streamlining to Nik that would accompany his solo career. Kershaw's photo reveals a different creature entirely from the styled pop star of 1984. His hair is unremarkably short, no hint of the architectural mullet to come. He wears a plain cotton long-sleeved shirt with casually rolled sleeves. While the photo itself is artistically composed – shot in black and white with Kershaw posed away from the camera, arm extended expressively – it's unmistakably pre-image, pre-stylist, pre-stardom. This is a team-effort musician in a team-effort band, no more or less important than his three colleagues.

The album's commercial prospects remain an intriguing what-if. Musically, it's sophisticated without being alienating, complex without being pretentious. But then there's that cover art – a black and white photograph of a British phone box with a man (visible only from torso down) lying supine at the bottom. The title is placed scrawled across the nearby wall in red handwriting, with 'You' underlined with a trailing red line that peters out ominously.

Was it meant to be darkly humorous? A visual gag about waiting so long for someone to call that you literally expire? Or did it read as something more sinister – self-harm, desperation, tragedy? The ambiguity recalls The Police's 'Can't Stand Losing You' single cover with its suicide imagery, but at least that matched the song's lyrical content. Fusion's upbeat, sophisticated music bore no relation to the potentially grim cover image. It's not unreasonable to wonder if this visual miscalculation hurt the album's chances – record shop browsers might have expected Joy Division and found themselves with jazz-funk instead.

The telephone theme extends to the album's release on Telephone Records, a label so obscure that research yields almost nothing about its origins or operations. It's entirely possible – though impossible to confirm – that this was essentially a vanity label created by the band themselves, another indicator of the project's small-scale ambitions. The back cover notes that "This album was recorded between April 1979 and May 1980," suggesting sessions grabbed when possible rather than the concentrated studio time of a major label production. Yet despite these apparently modest circumstances, nothing about the final product screams amateur hour. The recording quality is solid, the cover art professionally executed, the pressing clean. This contradiction – professional standards on what appears to be a shoestring operation – only deepens the mystery of Telephone Records and makes Fusion's sole album all the more intriguing as an artefact of Kershaw's pre-fame career.

Perhaps most importantly, the Fusion album demolishes any notion that Kershaw emerged from nowhere. There's a level of studio craft, performance confidence, musical sophistication – all clearly evident in 1980. When Mickey Modern received that demo tape a few years later, he wasn't hearing raw potential that needed development. He was hearing someone who'd already served a serious apprenticeship, who understood performance and arrangement at a near-professional level.

Fusion might have only produced one album, but it was foundational. Every collaborative moment, every extended instrumental, every genre experiment was preparation for what was to come. Kershaw honed his craft as part of an ensemble before becoming a solo star, understood democracy before accepting autocracy, explored multiple musical directions before choosing his path.

The distance between 'Look Behind You' and 'Human Racing' – between Fusion's jazz-funk-rock amalgam and Kershaw's synth-pop success – might seem vast. But listen closely and you hear the same musical intelligence, the same melodic gift, the same refusal to do the obvious. Fusion wasn't a false start; it was essential groundwork.

Third Time Lucky:
The Resurrection of a Nuclear Pop Classic

In recent interviews, Kershaw has reflected on a music industry that, to a point, once understood patience – a time when a single could struggle, struggle again, and still be given another shot at success. The journey of 'I Won't Let the Sun Go Down on Me' reads like a masterclass in persistent belief, both from artist and label.

First released in September 1983, the single landed with barely a whisper. MCA tried again in November with new sleeve art and a renewed promotional push. This time it scraped into the UK top one-hundred, spending eight weeks on the chart but stalling at number forty-seven. In today's streaming-dominated industry, where songs that don't explode within days are often abandoned along with their representative group or artist, this would be the end of the story. Delete, move on, next.

But 1983-84 was different. That number forty-seven position was viewed not as failure but as evidence of potential – a foothold rather than a gravestone. MCA saw those eight weeks in the lower reaches of the charts as proof that something was connecting, even if the connection wasn't yet strong enough to break through. Instead of cutting their losses, they doubled down.

The strategy paid off spectacularly. After 'Wouldn't It Be Good' crashed into the top five and 'Dancing Girls' secured another top twenty hit, MCA gave 'I Won't Let the Sun Go Down on Me' its third life in June 1984. This time, with Kershaw's name established and radio programmers primed, the song rocketed to number two. The single became one of his signature songs, proving that sometimes great songs just need to wait for their moment.

For fans of Kershaw's music, this persistence represents a narrow escape from an alternate timeline where one of his finest songs might have been relegated to obscurity. It also demonstrates that MCA understood what they had in Kershaw – not just a one-hit possibility but an artist worth nurturing, an investment that might require patience but would ultimately reward faith.

The song itself was perfectly calibrated for its historical moment. Written during the Cold War's paranoid final act, when Reagan and Andropov were trading rhetorical blows and the Doomsday Clock ticked ominously close to midnight, 'I Won't Let the Sun Go Down on Me' channelled nuclear anxiety through pop melody. The lyrics sparkle with satirical electricity: "Old men in stripy trousers rule the world with plastic smiles" wouldn't have looked out of place in a *Spitting Image* script, while "Forefinger on the button, is he blue or is he red?" reduced the fate of humanity to a question of political colour-coding.

Kershaw was initially coy about the song's apocalyptic undertones. He told *Number One* magazine in September 1984: "It's probably not immediately obvious but 'I Won't Let the Sun' is about The Bomb, or rather about people taking responsibility for what they do generally. It's saying that it probably won't do much good for one person to shout about these things but I'm going to anyway."

That "probably not immediately obvious" comment is classic Kershaw understatement. The song managed to be simultaneously a floor-filler and a warning siren, wrapping existential dread in such an irresistible package that people danced to their own potential annihilation. It was protest music that didn't sound like protest music, which might be why radio programmers who would have balked at anything overtly political embraced it so warmly.

The three-act drama of the single's release speaks to a different era's understanding of artist development. Today's industry might have condemned Kershaw to the algorithm's basement after that first failure. But in 1983-84, record labels understood that breaking an artist was a campaign, not a sprint. They recognised that sometimes the audience needs to be prepared for what you're offering, that timing can be everything, and that a song that fails in September might conquer the world by the following June.

The resurrection of 'I Won't Let the Sun Go Down on Me' wasn't just a commercial triumph; it was validation of a more thoughtful approach to the music business, one that understood that great songs don't always announce themselves immediately. Sometimes they need to knock three times before anyone answers the door.

Critical Misfires: When the Press Got It Wrong

It would be tempting to imagine that *Human Racing* emerged to universal acclaim in February 1984, carried aloft on a wave of critical enthusiasm that matched its eventual commercial success. The reality was rather more bruising. Some of the initial reviews read less like music criticism and more like character assassination.

Smash Hits, the magazine that would soon plaster Kershaw across its pages as he became a teen idol, awarded the album a devastating one star out of ten. Their reviewer dismissed it as "Competent but relentlessly dull synthesized meanderings of no importance to anyone but Mr Kershaw himself (and even he doesn't sound that interested)." They grudgingly acknowledged 'Wouldn't It Be Good' as providing "the one memorable moment" before delivering a final twist of the knife: the album was "notable only for making Howard Jones sound like Twisted Sister."

The sheer nastiness of the tone is striking – this wasn't criticism but cruelty, the sort of review that seems designed to wound rather than evaluate. The comparison to Howard Jones, already becoming tiresome, was weaponised here with particular venom. That *Smash Hits* would soon embrace Kershaw as one of their cover stars only emphasises how spectacularly wrong they got this initial assessment, and how fickle the music press could be when the wind changed direction.

Record Mirror was marginally less brutal but equally dismissive. Their reviewer acknowledged that "Nik has struck a chord with 'Wouldn't It Be Good'" before comparing the album's songs to "those shiny chrome things that turn to a dull green after a week or two's handling." The review went on to position Kershaw as "basically a singer/songwriter of the old school where people used to strum away at guitars, except that his tunes benefit from the embellishment of modern technology."

The critique continued with surgical precision: "The lyrics are too impersonal for this sort of music, which relies on a very personal approach, while the melodies don't have the verve of, say, Gary Numan's early arrangements to carry them through." Even when trying to identify highlights, the reviewer couldn't resist backhanded compliments. 'Drum Talk' was "probably" his most adventurous track, 'Bogart' was merely "ponderous," and both fell into "very obvious synthesizer tricks." The review's sole genuine praise was reserved for the title track, described as "the only song of real worth," before ending with a sarcastic flourish quoting Kershaw's own lyrics: "'They fill your heads with clever verses, and then disappear [sic].' How true, Nik, how true."

What's particularly fascinating about the *Record Mirror* review is its apparent disdain for the very technology that defined the era. Here we are in 1984, at the height of synth-pop's commercial and creative dominance, and the reviewer seems almost resentful that Kershaw isn't strumming an acoustic guitar. The dismissal of synthesizers as mere "embellishment" and "obvious tricks" feels bizarrely out of step with the musical moment. For anyone reading today, when electronic production is so thoroughly integrated into popular music that we barely notice it, this technological snobbery seems almost quaint.

Thankfully, these reviews proved about as predictive as a broken crystal ball. *Human Racing* would go on to achieve platinum status, spawn multiple hit singles, and establish Kershaw as one of the decade's defining artists. The public heard what the critics apparently couldn't – sophisticated pop songwriting that used technology not as a gimmick but as an integral part of its artistic expression.

These early reviews serve as valuable reminders that critical consensus and commercial success rarely arrive simultaneously. What seems like an unstoppable debut in hindsight often begins with scepticism, dismissal, or outright hostility from the gatekeepers. The critics who savaged *Human Racing* weren't just wrong about the album; they were wrong about where pop music was heading, wrong about what audiences wanted, and spectacularly wrong about Kershaw's significance to the decade's musical landscape.

That *Human Racing* survived and thrived despite such

initial critical brutality speaks to both the strength of the material and the ultimate irrelevance of professional tastemakers when an artist truly connects with an audience. Sometimes the critics are the last to know when something special has arrived.

A Nice Surprise from Across the Pond

By April 1984, American radio was beginning to pay attention. *Billboard*'s review of *Human Racing* offered a marked contrast to the British critical mauling, demonstrating that sometimes an ocean's distance provides better perspective. The American trade bible praised the album's "well-crafted dance-oriented pop and more traditional pop and rock elements," noting how Kershaw "Anglicizes its R&B strategies while supplying stronger songs than many techno pop debuts have offered in recent months." Their prediction that "mainstream rock formats will find strong tracks, as will pop and dance fans" proved prescient.

The album climbed to number seventy on the Billboard 200 – not earth-shattering, but respectable for a British artist who wasn't actively pursuing the American dream with the single-minded determination that had characterised the post-Beatles British invasion. This wasn't part of some grand strategic assault on America; Kershaw hadn't relocated to Los Angeles or tailored his sound for Midwestern radio. The recognition came organically, testament to music that transcended geographic boundaries even without a focused campaign. By 1985, he would be performing across the

Atlantic with increasing frequency, building on this unexpected foothold.

But it was back home and across Europe where *Human Racing* truly demonstrated its commercial muscle. Good reviews or bad, the public had spoken decisively. The album peaked at number five in the UK and crashed into the top ten in Germany, Finland, and Norway. In an era when British acts often struggled to translate beyond English-speaking territories, Kershaw was proving genuinely international.

The singles tell their own story of sustained success. 'Wouldn't It Be Good' reached number four, a bonafide smash. 'Dancing Girls' peaked at thirteen, another solid hit. 'I Won't Let the Sun Go Down on Me' justified its three releases by soaring to number two. Even 'Human Racing,' the fourth single, managed a respectable number nineteen. Four singles, four hits – a strike rate that would make any A&R executive weep with joy. The album finished 1984 as the year's twenty-second best-selling album in Britain, earned a Brit Award nomination for Best British Album, and was certified platinum by the BPI.

What's truly remarkable about *Human Racing*, however, is its depth of quality. This wasn't an album with four good songs and six fillers – every single track possessed single potential. This might sound like hyperbole, but consider the evidence. 'Drum Talk' throbs with a rhythmic intensity that would have ignited dancefloors; its intricate percussion programming and infectious groove could easily have followed 'Dancing Girls' into the charts. 'Shame on You' bounces with the kind of melodic confidence that radio programmers dream about, its hooks sharp enough to cut glass.

'Bogart' might move at a more measured pace, but its sophisticated arrangement and intriguing Humphrey Bogart metaphor would have made for a fascinating single release – thoughtful pop that trusted its audience's intelligence. 'Cloak and Dagger' strikes a perfect balance between dancefloor appeal and political commentary, its imagery sitting comfortably alongside 'I Won't Let the Sun Go Down on Me' in terms of topical relevance wrapped in irresistible melody.

Even the album tracks that might be considered "deep cuts" shimmer with single-worthy qualities. Each song is memorable, catchy, meaningful, and – crucially – possesses that replay value that separates great pop from the merely good. MCA could have randomly selected any track from *Human Racing*, released it as a single, and had a reasonable expectation of chart action.

This abundance of riches speaks to Kershaw's remarkable creative surge during this period. Many artists struggle to find four strong singles from an album; Kershaw had written ten potential hits and somehow corralled them into a cohesive whole. That *Smash Hits* heard "relentlessly dull meanderings" where millions heard pop perfection remains one of critical history's more spectacular misreadings.

The international success – from American radio to

German dancefloors to Scandinavian charts – proved that quality translates. *Human Racing* may not have been tailored for any specific market beyond the UK; it was simply excellent pop music that found its audience wherever it could be heard. The fact that it garnered attention across the pond without a calculated assault on America makes its achievement all the more impressive.

The Price of the Ride: Learning to Be Famous in Real Time

In 1984, Nik Kershaw's life transformed with the velocity of a jump cut. One moment he was Nicholas David Kershaw, unknown songwriter and musician from Suffolk; the next, he was 'Nik Kershaw,' splashed across the tabloids, a pop phenomenon. The shift wasn't gradual – it was seismic. Following *Human Racing*'s February release, Kershaw found himself strapped to a rocket he'd lit himself but couldn't quite control.

"Six months ago he was a nobody," marvelled one British tabloid, capturing the whiplash nature of pop stardom in the pre-internet age. Kershaw himself has reflected in recent interviews on the surreal blur of that year, admitting he was so busy living his dream that he forgot to actually experience it. The machinery of fame moved too fast for contemplation. German fans somehow acquired his parents' phone number and called to interrogate them about his school days. Disguises became necessary for simple errands. Young fans would chase him down the street, pulling at his clothes until the fabric tore – literal evidence of celebrity's grip.

This was the Faustian bargain of eighties pop stardom: your songs on every radio, your privacy in tatters. For someone of Kershaw's evident talent, it might have seemed a reasonable trade – taking the rough with the smooth, as they say – but the 'rough,' perhaps, might have been rougher than anyone could have prepared him for.

Perhaps most jarring was the crash course in performance that fame demanded. *Top of the Pops* wanted him centre stage, miming to 'Wouldn't It Be Good' for the nation. In recent interviews, he's been refreshingly honest about that baptism: handed a snood and fingerless gloves (the eighties demanded its props), placed before the cameras, and essentially told to figure it out as he went along. "Right, off you go," and suddenly you're a pop star, whether you know how to be one or not.

Today's artists, Kershaw notes, can attend training courses and performance workshops. But 1984 was still the Wild West of music television. *Top of the Pops* had a fresh look for the eighties; MTV was an American phenomenon barely three years old; the grammar of the music video was still being written. Everyone was making it up as they went along, but at least directors and producers could hide behind cameras. Kershaw had to improvise his pop star persona in real time, in front of millions.

The publicity machine presented its own peculiar challenges. Music journalists were one thing – at least they occasionally asked about chord progressions or lyrical inspiration. But the teen magazines were something else entirely, determined to package Kershaw as heartthrob material. This wasn't personal; it was simply how the industry monetised young male talent in 1984. Teen girls bought singles and posters and magazines, and the industry knew it. An artist's feelings about being transformed into bedroom wall decoration were largely irrelevant.

The styling itself became another layer of this commodification. Kershaw has spoken candidly about being styled – dressed up for the cameras, the bleached mullet that seemed to defy both gravity and reason. None of this was accidental; it was calculated image-making by professionals who understood that in 1984, you weren't just selling songs, you were selling a complete fantasy package. The clothes weren't meant to express Kershaw's personality – they were designed to make teenage hearts flutter and magazines fly off newsagent shelves.

This visual packaging was as meticulously crafted as any recording session. Stylists would arrive with racks of clothes that bore no resemblance to anything in Kershaw's own wardrobe. The brief was clear: create an image that was simultaneously accessible and aspirational, boyish but knowing, distinctive enough to stand out on *Top of the Pops* but safe enough for suburban bedrooms. The fact that Kershaw himself might have preferred something else was beside the point. He wasn't just plain old Nicholas anymore; he was a product line that happened to write exceptionally good songs.

The irony, of course, was that this manufactured image

often overshadowed the very real talent it was meant to promote. Here was a musician who could craft complex arrangements and clever lyrics, reduced in teen magazines to discussions of his favourite colour and preferred salad dressing. The image became more famous than the chord progressions; the hair more analysed than the harmonies. It was a bargain that many artists of that era had to make – submit to the styling, play the game, and hope that somewhere between the makeovers and photo shoots, people might actually listen to your music.

The banality of fame revealed itself in wonderful ways during live television appearances. *Saturday Superstore*'s phone-in segments became exercises in repetitive absurdity, with young caller after young caller asking Kershaw to wave at the camera and say hello to their Aunt Margaret or cousin Kevin. After the third or fourth request, Kershaw quipped that he might "run out of waves" – a perfectly pitched response that managed to be both funny and faintly desperate. This was children's live television in all its unfiltered glory, where quality control meant making sure nobody swore on air. The vetting process was so lax that a few years later, a caller would famously get through to *Going Live!* to ask Five Star why they were "so fucking crap" – yep, live on Saturday morning television.

More poignant were the moments when children seemed to seek something deeper from their pop heroes. When one young caller asked Kershaw if he'd been bullied at school, the question hung in the air like an uninvited confession. Kershaw navigated it deftly – explaining he'd used humour to defuse situations – but the moment was telling. This was pre-ChildLine Britain, where troubled kids might genuinely look to pop stars for guidance that should have come from elsewhere. The weight of that misplaced trust must have been extraordinary.

We're not suggesting Kershaw resented his success – only he knows the true texture of those experiences. But what's clear is that the scale and speed of his 1984 ascent required him to master an entire portfolio of skills nobody had warned him about. He'd wanted to be a successful musician; he'd become a phenomenon. The distance between those two things was vast, and he had to cross it at a sprint, in full public view, while trying not to trip over his own snood.

The remarkable thing isn't that the experience was overwhelming – it's that Kershaw navigated it with such apparent grace, producing a second album amid the chaos and maintaining his sanity while his privacy evaporated. He'd lit the rocket, true enough. But nobody had told him it would fly quite this fast, or this high, or that the view from up there would be quite so vertiginous.

The Quintessential Eighties Icon: From Unemployment Benefit Office to Pop Stardom

There's something beautifully, perfectly, irreducibly eighties about Nik Kershaw's origin story and image from that era. The trajectory from unemployment benefit office employee to pop star could only have happened in that specific moment of British cultural history. He'd left school midway through his A-levels, trading potential university prospects for a desk at the local unemployment office while pursuing music in his spare time. When Kershaw mentions this background in 1984 interviews, there's an almost poetic resonance to it – here was someone who'd literally worked in the epicentre of Thatcher's Britain's most visible crisis, processing the claims of the unemployed, before escaping to become one of the decade's defining success stories.

The unemployment benefit office detail feels loaded with meaning in retrospect. This was the Britain of 'Ghost Town' by The Specials, of riots in Brixton and Toxteth, of industries closing and dole queues lengthening. Thatcher's monetarist policies had sent unemployment soaring to levels not seen since the 1930s, and the benefit office had become a symbol of national malaise – captured brilliantly in *Boys from the Blackstuff* and countless angry punk songs. That Kershaw went from stamping signing-on cards to having his face on bedroom walls feels like the ultimate eighties transformation narrative.

His lyrics captured the political mood with surgical precision. "Old men in stripy trousers" from 'I Won't Let the Sun Go Down on Me' could have been describing the cabinet benches of Westminster circa 1984. With hindsight, the image seems to prefigure Rik Mayall's grotesque Tory MP Alan B'Stard in *The New Statesman*, though Kershaw's song predated Marks and Gran's savage satire by a few years. The whole package – the political anxiety, the nuclear dread, the sense of being governed by out-of-touch elites – feels like the concentrated essence of eighties Britain.

The Mayall connection runs deeper than coincidental imagery. When asked during a *Saturday Superstore* phone-in about his favourite comedians, Kershaw named John Cleese and Rik Mayall – the latter having established himself as a highly respected alternative comedian through his anarchic work on *The Young Ones*. In a delightful bit of cosmic scheduling, the universe had delivered two of Britain's eighties icons within the same week in March 1958: Kershaw on the 1st, Mayall on the 7th. Both would spend the eighties creating work that defined the decade, albeit in very different mediums.

Then there's the hair – because you can't discuss eighties Kershaw without discussing The Hair. From 1984 to 1985, his mullet seemed to develop its own gravitational field, growing bigger, more elaborate, more architecturally ambitious with each appearance. At one point, highlights were added to the construction, though Kershaw later admitted he'd had to abandon them when they started causing his hair to fall out – even follicles have their limits. The hairstyle became so iconic that it's now impossible to imagine eighties Kershaw without it – as essential to his image as the snood or the fingerless gloves.

What's fascinating is how completely this eighties incarnation of Kershaw has been preserved in cultural amber. Despite a career that has continued productively for over four decades, despite numerous albums and evolution as an artist, the image that immediately springs to mind when his name is mentioned remains that young man with the gravity-defying hair. He's been time-capsuled at that exact moment of peak eighties-ness.

This preservation isn't diminishing – if anything, it's testament to how perfectly Kershaw embodied his moment. He wasn't trying to look or sound like the eighties; he simply was the eighties, from his unemployment benefit office backstory to his political anxieties to his magnificent mullet. While he's continued to create and evolve as an artist, that captured moment from 1984-85 remains iconic precisely because it was so authentic to its time.

In an era of manufactured nostalgia and calculated retro styling, there's something powerful about an artist who was simply, genuinely, unconsciously of their moment. Kershaw didn't set out to become an eighties icon – he was just a talented musician from Suffolk who happened to crystallise an entire decade's aesthetic and anxieties into pop perfection. The fact that we're still talking about that hair, those lyrics, that journey from benefit office employee to *Top of the Pops*, proves that sometimes the most enduring cultural artefacts are the ones that weren't trying to be timeless at all.

The Comparison That Wouldn't Quit: Nik Kershaw, Howard Jones, and Journalistic Shorthand

Throughout 1984, music journalists seemed incapable of mentioning Nik Kershaw without invoking Howard Jones in the same breath, as if the two were cosmic twins separated at birth and reunited by Roland synthesizers. On the surface, the comparison was almost lazy in its obviousness: two British solo artists, both crafting intelligent pop music in an era often dismissed as superficial, both achieving massive commercial success within months of each other.

But look closer and the comparison reveals something more interesting about the musical moment they shared. Both Kershaw and Jones represented a particular evolution in British pop – the singer-songwriter as complete auteur, using technology not as a crutch but as an orchestra. These weren't manufactured stars backed by anonymous session musicians; they were architects of their own sound, building entire worlds from keyboards and drum machines.

The temporal overlap only added fuel to the

comparative fire. Jones had actually fired the first shot with the release of 'New Song' in August 1983, establishing his presence before Kershaw emerged. When *Human's Lib* arrived in March 1984 – just one month after Kershaw's *Human Racing* – the coincidence of two 'Human' albums from keyboard-wielding solo artists was almost too perfect for journalists to resist.

In response to the publication's question as to whether he was "MCA's answer to Howard Jones," Kershaw told *Record Mirror* in March 1984, "I know his album is called *Human's Lib* and mine is called *Human Racing*, but that's just a coincidence. We just happen to be solo artists and that's all there is to it. I had a brief chat with him recently, he's a lovely fellah." Never mind that the shared word was pure coincidence; the press had found their narrative and weren't letting go.

But anyone who actually listened to both albums would recognise them as entirely different species. Howard Jones' 'Conditioning,' 'What is Love?' and 'Pearl in the Shell' are completely different songs worthy of their own time and attention, each exploring distinct musical and lyrical territory. Meanwhile, Kershaw was crafting his own unique sonic world with tracks like 'Wouldn't It Be Good' and 'Dancing Girls.' Both artists deserved attention for their sophisticated approach to pop architecture. They were both proving that electronic pop could be thoughtful without being pretentious, complex without losing its essential accessibility.

The comparison did both artists a disservice by

suggesting they were somehow interchangeable – two settings on the same machine. This was patently absurd. Jones' vocals had a distinctive breathiness; Kershaw's delivery could shift from yearning to sardonic within a single verse. Their melodic sensibilities, their harmonic choices, their very approach to constructing a pop song – all were distinctly their own.

Yet this divergence is precisely what made both artists essential to 1984's musical landscape. They proved that synthesizer-based pop could carry any message, support any worldview, express any emotion beyond the "cold" and "mechanical" criticisms often levelled at electronic music.

What united them, beyond their tools and their timing, was their insistence on creativity in an industry that typically preferred its artists compartmentalised. Both wrote, arranged, and performed their material. Both understood that the new technology wasn't just about new sounds alone – it was about utilising it for songs that offered real melodic and emotional resonance.

Looking back from our current vantage point, where laptop productions dominate the charts and the solo electronic artist is the norm rather than the exception, both Kershaw and Jones appear as essential transitional figures. They helped establish the template that everyone from Calvin Harris to Billie Eilish would later follow: the artist as autonomous creative entity, beholden to no band dynamics, no session musician schedules, no external arrangers.

That they were so often lumped together says more about the critics' need for simple narratives than any real artistic similarity. But perhaps being misunderstood together was better than being misunderstood alone. In 1984, both Nik Kershaw and Howard Jones were creating intelligent, emotionally sophisticated electronic pop music that trusted its audience to think while they danced. That they did so in entirely different ways only enriches the story of that remarkable musical moment. They weren't two versions of the same thing – they were parallel demonstrations that electronic pop music could be anything its creators imagined.

Surprising Influences in Rock

It would be tempting to imagine that the synthesizer pioneers of the eighties emerged from some cultural vacuum, fully formed with their drum machines, untouched by the decades of rock that preceded them. The reality is far more interesting. Every artist carries their early musical experiences forward, and Nik Kershaw – despite his association with gleaming eighties production – was very much a product of the guitar heroes who came before.

In a recent interview, Kershaw revealed something that might surprise those who know him only through 'The Riddle' or 'Wouldn't It Be Good': in his youth, he would sit and meticulously study Ritchie Blackmore's Deep Purple-era guitar solos. On the surface, this seems almost absurd – what could the synthesized pop perfection of 1984's *Human Racing* possibly have in common with the Hammond-organ-and-Marshall-stack assault of *Machine Head*?

Look closer, though, and the connection becomes not just plausible but logical. Blackmore was never just a rock guitarist; he was a musical magpie, incorporating modal melodies from folk traditions, baroque flourishes from classical music, and Eastern scales into what ostensibly fell under the banner of hard rock. His solos weren't just displays of technical prowess but compositional statements that drew from centuries of musical tradition. Sound familiar? As we'll explore in the detailed musical analysis later in this book, Kershaw's melodic sensibilities reveal exactly the same kind of broad influences – folk progressions hiding inside pop songs, harmonic curiosities dressed up as chart hits.

This shared approach to composition – the willingness to raid music history's entire cupboard rather than limiting oneself to genre conventions – links Blackmore and Kershaw far more meaningfully than their surface sounds might suggest. Both understood that a good melody is a good melody, whether it's played on a Stratocaster through a wall of Marshalls or programmed into a Fairlight CMI.

Which brings us to something crucial that often gets overlooked: Kershaw is a genuinely brilliant guitarist. This isn't hyperbole or fan enthusiasm – watch any live footage from 1984-85 and you'll see someone who could hold his own with any of the era's six-string heroes. For instance, the guitar solo in 'Wide Boy' isn't just competent; it's fluid, musical, and perfectly constructed. When Kershaw performs live today, over four decades later, it's still with a guitar in his hands, fingers dancing across the fretboard with the confidence that comes from genuine mastery.

In many ways, Kershaw's guitar prowess has been overshadowed by his association with electronic music. We tend to celebrate musicians who are known for one thing – Hendrix equals guitar, Elton equals piano, Phil Collins equals drums. Multi-instrumentalists sometimes have their individual instrumental abilities overlooked in favour of discussing their overall artistry. But make no mistake: if Kershaw had chosen to be "just" a guitarist, he had the chops to compete with anyone.

This rock foundation explains something essential about why Kershaw's electronic pop has endured. Underneath the period production lies solid musical architecture acquired from studying the masters. Those Blackmore solos were a masterclass in tension and release, about how to build to a climax, about the importance of melody over mere technique. These lessons translate regardless of instrument – a keyboard part can breathe and bend and wail just like a guitar if the person creating it understands what makes music move.

The divide between the guitar-based seventies and synth-dominated eighties was always more about technology than musical philosophy. Artists like Kershaw proved that you could honour your influences while embracing new tools, that a Deep Purple fan could become a synth-pop star without betraying either identity. He didn't abandon the guitar for keyboards; he added them to his arsenal, approaching them with the same musical intelligence he'd developed studying Blackmore's fretwork.

In the end, great musicians transcend their instruments. Kershaw learnt from listening to rock's guitar gods not just how to play, but how to think about music, how to construct solos that served the song, how to bring disparate influences together into something cohesive. That his canvas varied in instrumentation doesn't diminish the artistry – if anything, it demonstrates its versatility.

(Of course, it would be reductive to suggest that Blackmore was Kershaw's only or even primary influence. Kershaw has spoken with equal enthusiasm about a diverse roster of musical heroes, including Jeff Beck, Rick Wakeman, and Elton John. What's significant about the Blackmore connection isn't that it was exclusive, but that it exemplifies Kershaw's broader approach to musical exploration – studying the greats across all genres. This omnivorous musical appetite, this refusal to be confined by genre boundaries, would become one of the defining characteristics of his own work.)

The Riddle of The Riddle:
When Commerce and Creativity Collide

The story of how *The Riddle* album came to exist reveals the perpetual tension between artistic idealism and commercial reality that defines the modern music industry. In recent interviews, Kershaw has been remarkably candid about the circumstances surrounding his second album's creation, painting a picture of an artist caught between the demands of the marketplace and the needs of the creative process.

MCA wanted to strike while the iron was hot – and in 1984, Kershaw's iron was practically molten. With *Human Racing* still climbing charts worldwide, the label pushed for a follow-up in time for the crucial Christmas market. This commercial imperative, Kershaw has since reflected, created a problematic knock-on effect: rushing to deliver *The Riddle* by November 1984 meant a longer, more damaging gap before his third album, *Radio Musicola* (released in October 1986). The irony is palpable – in trying to maintain momentum, the label may have inadvertently disrupted it.

A glance at Kershaw's 1984 schedule reveals the almost absurd conditions under which *The Riddle* was created.

The album had to be written, recorded, and delivered for a November release – all while the dust from *Human Racing*'s success had barely settled (Kershaw undertook a promotional tour from late March to early July, with most dates in the UK and a small handful in Europe). The pressure was immense: following up a debut that had already set the bar incredibly high, with the clock ticking relentlessly. Yes, he mentioned during a phone-in on *Saturday Superstore* that he could typically write a song in two to three hours, but there's a world of difference between having three hours of creative freedom and having to produce on demand while the label executives tap their watches. The commercial machinery didn't pause for artistic contemplation – it demanded product, and it demanded it now.

One small advantage in the race against time was that a version of 'Wide Boy' had originally been recorded for *Human Racing* but dropped before the album's release. Kershaw remarked that by the time it appeared on *The Riddle* it was "an old song, probably four or five years old." Having this track already partially developed must have provided some breathing room in the schedule, yet this hardly negates the overall time crunch. However, the fact that Kershaw could slot in an older track and have it sit seamlessly alongside newly written material speaks to the consistency of his songwriting.

Here's where the story becomes even more fascinating: *The Riddle* isn't just good – it's exceptional. Under circumstances that might have produced a rushed, half-baked cash-in, Kershaw delivered an album that some consider superior to his debut. Perhaps the pressure and exhaustion of 1984 pushed his creativity into overdrive, forcing him to trust his instincts rather than overthink. Or perhaps we're simply witnessing what happens when an artist hits that rare sweet spot where talent, opportunity, and urgency align perfectly. We'll never know what a more leisurely-paced second album might have sounded like – whether it would have been even better given time to breathe, or whether it might have meandered without the focusing pressure of a deadline.

The most telling artefact of this rushed creation is the title track itself, which has become perhaps the most famous song about nothing in pop history. The lyrics that so many have attempted to decode – that song that launched infinite theories – were never meant to exist at all. They were placeholder gibberish, musical Lorem Ipsum that Kershaw fully intended to replace with "proper" words once he found the time. But time was the one thing MCA's schedule didn't allow, and when someone suggested they could just leave the nonsense lyrics and call it 'The Riddle,' a piece of pop folklore was born.

The beautiful accident of 'The Riddle' reveals something profound about how we engage with pop music. Those meaningless words – "Near a tree by a river there's a hole in the ground" – somehow sounded exactly right, their cryptic non-meaning becoming more intriguing than any deliberate message could have been. Letters poured in from fans convinced they'd cracked the code. When a young viewer phoned *Saturday Superstore* to ask what it all meant, Kershaw played along brilliantly, claiming he couldn't reveal the answer as he was about to tour internationally and didn't want to spoil the surprise for fans abroad.

This playful mystification became part of the song's appeal, turning a time-saving compromise into a marketing masterstroke. The ambiguity that resulted from having no time to write "real" lyrics created more engagement than clarity ever could have. It's a perfect metaphor for the album itself – something that shouldn't have worked given the circumstances, but somehow worked beautifully.

Today, Kershaw freely admits that 'The Riddle' means nothing at all, that its lyrics are purely phonetic furniture arranged to complement the melody. But in a way, that admission only deepens the song's appeal. It stands as proof that in pop music, how something sounds can matter more than what it says, that the feeling of meaning can be more powerful than meaning itself. The fact that this discovery was forced by commercial pressures rather than artistic choice makes it even more delicious – sometimes the best creative decisions are the ones you don't have time to make.

Music First, Words to Follow

While it would be presumptuous to claim every Nik Kershaw composition followed an identical blueprint, evidence reveals a clear pattern in his creative process: the music often came first, with lyrics fitted to the melodic framework like words to a crossword puzzle already drawn.

'The Riddle' stands as the most famous example of this approach, its nonsense lyrics achieving immortality through pure sonic compatibility. But it wasn't an isolated case. Take 'Don Quixote,' another track from Kershaw's second album. During an appearance on *Saturday Live* in July 1985, Kershaw revealed the arbitrary nature of even his more supposedly meaningful lyrics with characteristic wit. The title phrase 'Don Quixote,' he joked, could just as easily have been 'Gorgonzola' – it was simply a matter of finding syllables that scanned correctly against the melody.

The admission is both hilarious and revealing. Here was a song ostensibly about Cervantes' legendary knight-errant, and Kershaw cheerfully admitted he might have written an ode to Italian cheese if the phonetics had worked. It gets better: when pressed about the literary inspiration, Kershaw confessed that he didn't fancy reading a book as big as Cervantes' masterpiece. His solution? He got his wife to read the doorstop of a tome and provide him with a digest version suitable for pop song adaptation. It's the sort of creative pragmatism that would horrify purists but perfectly captures the working reality of a pop craftsman under pressure.

This approach – melodic architecture first, semantic meaning second – might seem backwards to those who imagine songwriters as poets who then set their words to music. But for Kershaw, working in the pressure cooker of 1984, it was both practical and inspired. The melody told him what the words needed to sound like; the meaning could be negotiated afterwards. Sometimes, as with 'The Riddle,' the meaning never arrived at all, and the song was arguably better for it. Other times, as with 'Don Quixote,' a theme would be retrofitted to the existing sonic structure, creating the illusion of literary depth through what was essentially an elaborate game of syllabic Tetris.

This isn't to diminish Kershaw's lyrical abilities – when he had a message to convey, as in 'I Won't Let the Sun Go Down on Me' or 'Wouldn't It Be Good,' his words could be sharp, evocative, and meaningful. But the music-first approach reveals something important about his priorities as a pop craftsman: the sound was sovereign. Everything else, even meaning itself, was negotiable.

A (Slightly) Warmer Reception from the Critics

After the critical mauling that greeted *Human Racing*, *The Riddle* found the press in a marginally more generous mood – though 'marginal' is doing heavy lifting here. *Smash Hits*, who had awarded the debut a devastating one star out of ten, managed to locate six and a half stars for the follow-up, calling it "a commendable offering from the thinking person's Limahl."

Let that comparison sink in for a moment. Limahl and Kajagoogoo had given us 'Too Shy' and 'Ooh to Be Ah' – genuinely enjoyable hits that anyone who loves eighties music likely still plays with affection. But by 1984, the music press had decided that Limahl represented a certain kind of pop they considered frivolous – all style, no substance. To call Kershaw "the thinking person's Limahl" was *Smash Hits* trying to have their cake and eat it too. They were suggesting Kershaw was making the same kind of accessible pop music (which they clearly saw as somewhat beneath them), just with a few more brain cells involved. It was damning with the faintest of praise, positioning Kershaw as someone making intelligent music for people who still, fundamentally, enjoyed what the critics considered lightweight pop. The comparison reveals more about critical snobbery than about either artist's actual merits.

The review continued with observations about Kershaw being "very keen to be seen as the Jack of all trades, sometimes slickly funky or bubblingly poppy then, suddenly, out and out heavy." Whether this comment on versatility was meant as praise or criticism remains ambiguous – perhaps deliberately so. Yes, Kershaw could do multiple things, but was that breadth or lack of focus? The reviewer hedged their bets, noting it was "all excellently played" with "that familiar silver sheen production."

Record Mirror took a different tack, opening with faux sympathy: "Poor Nik Kershaw. He'd find life a lot easier if he had the matinee idol eyes of Quasimodo, a complexion with more eruptions than Mount Etna and the sumptuous figure of Big Daddy." The suggestion that Kershaw's good looks were somehow hampering critical appreciation was novel, if slightly bizarre. According to this logic, his "cuddly appeal of a Cabbage Patch Doll crossed with the puppy of the Andrex ads" was blinding people to his genuine talent.

The review diagnosed Kershaw with "follow-upitis – a serious complaint where a punishing schedule and heavy success impair the senses." They acknowledged his "excellent singles" that combined "the ruthless efficiency of a Mafia hitman with the chilling chart accuracy of a pop Robin Hood," possibly the most tortured metaphor in music journalism history. The verdict? "Not a bad album" but "not sharp enough," with a "rushed feel" that "won't disappoint fans" but left the reviewer expecting "more thought."

This sense of the album feeling rushed wasn't entirely unfair – Kershaw himself has acknowledged the pressure to deliver *The Riddle* for the Christmas market. But calling it "not sharp enough" seems almost perverse when discussing an album containing songs as precisely crafted as 'Wide Boy' and 'The Riddle.'

American critics proved more straightforward. *Billboard* noted that Kershaw's second album arrived "buoyed by a tidal wave of attention in his homeland" and praised his "egalitarian regard for the old verities of rhythm, melody and harmony." They singled out 'Wide Boy' and 'The Riddle' as the strongest tracks – no backhanded compliments about thinking persons' Limahls, no tortured metaphors about Robin Hood, just acknowledgment of solid pop craftsmanship.

For most Kershaw fans, these reviews remain baffling. *The Riddle* contains some of the most sophisticated pop music of the eighties. The album showcases superior songwriting and melodic invention that most artists would kill for. That it received such lukewarm notices says more about critical expectations than musical quality.

Fortunately, the buying public ignored the reviews entirely. *The Riddle* peaked at number eight in the UK, reached the top ten in New Zealand and Norway, and spawned three significant hits: 'The Riddle' (number three), 'Wide Boy' (number nine), and 'Don Quixote' (number ten). The album earned platinum certification from the BPI, proving that commercial success remains the best revenge against critical indifference.

Even if the album did feel rushed – to Kershaw, to some critics – the commercial results speak volumes. More importantly, *The Riddle*'s enduring appeal over forty years later suggests that those hurried 1984 studio sessions produced something far more lasting than anyone realised at the time. Sometimes the best work comes not from endless deliberation but from trusting your instincts when time is short and pressure is high.

The critics wanted more (as they saw it) thought; the public just wanted more Kershaw. Guess who won that argument.

Vision and Video:
The Visual Language of Kershaw's Success

For most of the 1980s, there were only four television channels to choose from – BBC1, BBC2, the regional ITV variant, and Channel 4 (which launched in November 1982). British viewer access to music videos was scarce. The weekly ration of music programming was slim, meaning many fans who bought Kershaw's records and read about him in *Smash Hits* might never have seen the elaborate visual worlds created for his singles. *Top of the Pops* was likely his most reliable television showcase, its weekly Thursday evening slot providing rare consistency in an era before YouTube made everything accessible at will.

Yet Kershaw's music videos, now easily viewable online, reveal another dimension of the Kershaw phenomenon – the scale of investment, both creative and financial, that went into establishing him as a complete audiovisual package.

The 'Dancing Girls' video translates the song's narrative literally but playfully. Kershaw plays a suited wage slave awakening to his alarm clock, trudging through streets where everyone else – housewives, policemen, a ballerina – dances with co-ordinated joy. The boardroom scene where an older female colleague transforms into a ballerina atop the conference table captures the song's escapist fantasy perfectly. It's fun, accessible, and reinforces the single's themes without pretension.

'Human Racing' features prison scenes of inmates playing board games, suggesting competition and confinement. Kershaw performs from a chair in a dark room surrounded by television screens. Neon-lit corridors, angular shapes, and isolation create an appropriately dystopian atmosphere. The image of Kershaw sitting with his knees to his chin while singing – vulnerable despite the technological surroundings – adds unexpected emotional depth.

'I Won't Let the Sun Go Down on Me' required two videos, reflecting its commercial journey. The original, filmed at Allington Castle in Kent, showed Kershaw on hillsides and in castle settings. When the single's third release finally caught fire in June 1984, a hurried "live" performance video was shot to capitalise on the momentum – Kershaw was too busy with European promotion for anything more elaborate. This visual evolution mirrors the song's own path of slow build to triumph.

Storm Thorgerson, the Hipgnosis designer responsible for Pink Floyd's iconic album covers, directed several of Kershaw's most memorable videos. His 'Wouldn't It Be Good' presents a visual masterpiece using primitive green-screen-type effects. Kershaw's white suit becomes a canvas for projected images – lined-up shoes, arguing couples – while he wanders a house filled with isolated figures. The narrative climaxes with Kershaw outside the building, surrounded by people all miming the song's chorus back at him, before he flees to a field where a satellite dish beams him away entirely. It's otherworldly, thought-provoking, and perfectly matched to the song's themes of mutual envy and disconnection.

'The Riddle,' directed by Thorgerson, embraces the absurdity of promoting meaningless lyrics. Kershaw slides into a room of surreal encounters – walls with protruding lips, drawers full of cakes and rats, a bald man with rats on his head. Whether this enhances or distracts from the song is debatable, but it certainly commits to the mystery, giving visual nonsense to match the lyrical variety. Some of the video's imagery draws inspiration from *Alice in Wonderland* – a descent into a world where logic dissolves and everything seems to hum with secret intent. But whether or not the viewer recognises that reference hardly matters; the sense of disorientation works on its own terms.

'Wide Boy,' directed by Thorgerson, presents an elaborate time-travel narrative. Beginning with a dishevelled, unshaven Kershaw seeing himself on an NME cover, the video whisks through decades of imagined fame – 1950s teddy boy, 1960s pop star, 1970s excess – before confronting him with the consequences of such a life. The production values are cinema-quality, the storytelling sophisticated.

'Don Quixote,' directed by Thorgerson and filmed in La Mancha, Spain ("It was very hot – too hot, in fact," Kershaw told *Saturday Live*), throws everything at the screen: windmills, flamenco dancers, knights on horseback, paint splashing through the air. Kershaw's mullet, by now reaching impressive proportions, flows dramatically in the Spanish wind.

These weren't cheap, quickly-shot promos but substantial productions with proper budgets and thoughtfully crafted narratives. They reveal Kershaw as a capable actor who could carry these visual stories with conviction – no small feat for someone who'd admitted uncertainty when first facing *Top of the Pops* cameras. More significantly, they demonstrate the level of investment MCA were making in establishing him as a complete artist, not just a voice on vinyl.

For those who missed these videos during their scattered original broadcasts, they now serve as time capsules of both Kershaw's artistic ambitions and the music industry's golden age of video investment. Watching them today, one gets a fuller picture of just how comprehensively Kershaw was being packaged and promoted – and how hard he was working, shooting elaborate videos between tours, recordings, and interviews. The videos represent days of his already crammed schedule, further evidence of the relentless pace at which his career was moving.

The videos weren't just promotional tools – they were artistic statements in their own right, adding layers of meaning (or deliberate meaninglessness) to songs that already worked perfectly well without visual accompaniment. That Kershaw and his team invested such effort in these productions, even when many fans might never see them, speaks to a commitment to excellence that extended beyond just the music. In the pre-MTV UK, these videos were ambitious gambles. Today, they're essential documents of pop at its most creatively confident.

The Weight of Wembley: Kershaw at Live Aid

By July 1985, Nik Kershaw had earned his place in British pop's inner circle. When Bob Geldof came calling for Live Aid, it wasn't a question of whether Kershaw belonged on that stage – he was essential casting. The night before the concert, they were interviewed together on *Wogan*, two men preparing for what would become one of television history's most-watched events. The build-up must have been extraordinary, the weight of expectation growing heavier with each passing hour.

At 2:22pm on 13th July, following Elvis Costello's rousing take on The Beatles' 'All You Need is Love,' Kershaw took the stage at Wembley. His setlist was a greatest hits in miniature: 'Wide Boy,' 'Don Quixote,' 'The Riddle,' and closing with 'Wouldn't It Be Good.' Four songs to represent himself before 72,000 people in the stadium and an estimated 1.9 billion watching worldwide. No pressure, then.

According to comments he's made in relatively recent years, what happened next went on to haunt Kershaw for a long time. But it shouldn't have. By any objective measure, his performance was strong – energetic, charismatic, vocally assured. His guitar solo on 'Wide Boy' flowed with confidence. But during 'Wouldn't It Be Good,' panic struck. The words vanished from his mind, and in that terrible moment of blankness, he defaulted to singing an earlier verse's lyrics. For Kershaw, who had crafted the song as a carefully structured conversation between different voices, each verse representing a new person explaining that the grass isn't greener, this repetition felt catastrophic. He's since described feeling "out of my depth" and like he was "standing on the shoulders of giants."

Here's the thing, though: almost nobody noticed. Watch the footage today and you'll see a professional delivering a professional performance. Unless you're a hardcore fan who knows the lyrics by heart, the "mistake" is invisible. The crowd didn't falter, the energy didn't dip, the world kept spinning. But for Kershaw, that moment crystallised into something larger – impostor syndrome made manifest before nearly two billion people.

Even the minor stumble at the beginning of 'Don Quixote' – he appears to trip on a cable but recovers with such fluidity it almost looks choreographed – becomes part of the performance's charm rather than a flaw. The Live Aid stage was notorious for its chaos, with equipment being swapped between acts at breakneck speed, cables everywhere, monitors that might or might not work. That Kershaw navigated this obstacle course while maintaining his performance speaks to his professionalism, not any lack thereof.

It's worth noting what wasn't played that day. 'I Won't

Let the Sun Go Down on Me' would have been symbolically perfect for the occasion – a song about anxiety caused by those in power repurposed for global charity. 'Human Racing' could have been an additional welcome to the set. That Kershaw had such strong material in reserve after barely eighteen months of success – that he could leave genuine hits unplayed and still deliver a set of wall-to-wall bangers – testifies to the extraordinary creative surge of his 1984 output.

The tragedy isn't that Kershaw fumbled some lyrics at Live Aid; it's that he spent years unable to watch footage of what was actually a triumph. Here was a young artist, barely two years into his mainstream career, holding his own on a bill that included Queen, Bowie, McCartney, and The Who. He didn't just survive; he delivered. The fact that he couldn't see this – that the internal critic drowned out the external evidence – reveals something profound about the burden of pressure that often accompanies genuine artistry.

Perhaps time has finally offered perspective. The Live Aid performance stands as a document of an artist at his commercial peak, confident enough to own that massive stage even while privately wrestling with doubt. That tension – between the polished exterior and the internal uncertainty – might actually be what made the performance so compelling. Perfect performances are forgettable; it's the human moments, the tiny cracks in the façade, that make something real.

Besides, in the broader context of Live Aid – a day when Paul McCartney's microphone failed completely, when dozens of acts wrestled with dodgy monitors and hastily assembled equipment, when stage crews scrambled to accommodate wildly different technical requirements with mere minutes between sets – forgetting a verse while still delivering a vocally and musically solid performance barely registers as a glitch. Kershaw belonged on that stage, even if it might have taken him decades to believe it.

Live at The Ritz:
Kershaw Commands New York

The performance captured at New York's Ritz on 13th April 1985 offers a masterclass in how to translate studio sophistication to the live stage. Opening with 'Cloak and Dagger,' Kershaw immediately establishes himself as more than just a studio artist. His vocals match the record's precision until the "We know what you're doing..." section, where something fascinating happens – the almost percussive studio delivery transforms into pure theatre. The words become dramatic, emphatic, carried by gesture as much as melody. Here's an artist who's learnt to inhabit his songs physically, putting a finger to his lips for "Mum's the word," spinning in circles during guitar solos, turning what could have been a straightforward reproduction into genuine performance art.

The transition to 'The Riddle' reveals clever stagecraft. The military-style drumming that opens the track extends longer in the live setting – not self-indulgence but practical showmanship, giving Kershaw time to switch guitars while maintaining momentum. It's the kind of professional detail that separates touring artists from studio purists, showing someone who understands both his equipment and his audience's attention.

What's remarkable about Kershaw's performance of 'The Riddle' is how he commits to storytelling despite knowing the lyrics are nonsense. He traces circles in the air for "around and around," throws mock punches for "never, never fight," draws hearts for "valentine." The audience doesn't know they're watching someone perform meaningless placeholder lyrics – and it doesn't matter. Kershaw delivers them as if they contain profound truth, proving that performance conviction can create meaning where none exists.

'Wide Boy' arrives with Kershaw's introduction that it's getting "quite a bit of airplay" stateside – understated British modesty. The guitar work here is exemplary, every solo note landing exactly where it should.

For 'Human Racing,' Kershaw abandons the guitar entirely, transforming the song into something approaching musical theatre. Standing on one leg and drawing a circle in the air for "paper moon," stalking across the stage for "there's a man," turning his head sharply for "look behind you" – this could be a lost number from a West End production. For someone who claimed uncertainty when the *Top of the Pops* cameras first rolled, he's become a remarkably assured physical performer.

The introduction to 'Wouldn't It Be Good' showcases Kershaw the crowd-worker. "We're not gonna start this song until I can see everybody's hands up in the air," he announces, adding with mock menace, "If there's someone next to you [not participating], give them a good kick for me, yeah?" His British accent probably added extra charm for the American audience – that distinctive sound that makes UK acts exotic in the States.

When that opening guitar riff finally arrives, the crowd erupts. By April 1985, this song had clearly embedded itself in American consciousness. The audience sings along to "don't wanna be here no more" – audible proof of connection, of songs transcending their origins to become communal property.

The set closes with 'I Won't Let the Sun Go Down on Me,' Kershaw demonstrating his multi-instrumental facility by starting at the keyboards before returning to guitar. The tempo's slightly faster than the record – not sloppiness but intention, adding celebratory energy to the finale. He performs searching gestures during "searching for an enemy," maintaining theatrical commitment to the very end.

What's striking throughout is the fidelity to the recorded versions. Apart from those dramatised spoken sections in 'Cloak and Dagger,' Kershaw delivers his songs as the audience knows them. This isn't about ego-driven reinterpretation or jazz-fusion noodling; it's about giving people what they came for while adding just enough visual theatre to make it special. It's professional, polished, reliable – qualities that might sound tame but take considerable skill to achieve night after night.

Consider the timing: this Ritz performance occurred exactly three months before Live Aid. Watching this New York show, you see an artist absolutely ready for Wembley's global stage. The crowd engagement, the musical precision, the theatrical flourishes, the multi-instrumental confidence – all the elements are there. The American audience responding so enthusiastically to a British synth-pop artist proves that Kershaw's appeal was genuinely international.

The Ritz performance dismantles any notion that Kershaw was merely a studio artist who couldn't deliver live. Here's someone who understood that live performance isn't just about reproducing the record – it's about creating an experience that honours the songs while adding dimensions that only physical presence can provide. Every guitar solo, every theatrical gesture, every moment of crowd interaction shows an artist who had evolved from demo tape hopeful to convincing performer.

That evolution would be tested three months later at Live Aid, but watching the Ritz footage now, the outcome seems inevitable. This wasn't someone out of his depth; this was an artist hitting his stride, ready for whatever stage the world could offer.

Under the Bonnet: The Musical Architecture of Kershaw's Songs

Pop music criticism often stops at the surface – is it catchy, does it sound good, will it sell? But truly understanding why certain songs endure while others evaporate requires looking deeper, past the production sheen and into the musical machinery underneath. The following analysis examines every track from *Human Racing* and *The Riddle* through the lens of music theory, not to diminish their immediate pleasures but to illuminate why these pleasures are so expertly constructed.

What we'll discover is that Kershaw wasn't just writing catchy tunes – he was building sophisticated musical structures that reward close examination. Behind those accessible melodies lie unexpected chord progressions borrowed from jazz, modulations that shouldn't work but do, rhythmic complexities disguised as simple pop beats, harmonic tensions that create emotional effects listeners can feel even if they can't name them.

This isn't about academic gatekeeping or suggesting you need a music degree to enjoy 'Wouldn't It Be Good.' These songs already work on a visceral level – millions of listeners have proven that. But understanding the craft beneath the catchiness reveals another layer of Kershaw's artistry. What's the magic behind the music?

The answers lie in specific musical choices – a space in the arrangement here, a chromatic descent there, a deceptive cadence that sends the melody somewhere unexpected. Kershaw was smuggling jazz harmony into the charts, using compositional techniques that most pop writers either didn't know or didn't dare employ. He understood that complexity and accessibility aren't enemies – they can be dance partners, each making the other more interesting.

Consider this section a guided tour through the engine room of some of the eighties' finest pop music. We'll examine how Kershaw builds tension and release, how he uses harmony and instrumentation to create unexpected colours, how his bass lines do far more than just mark time. We'll see how – whether through formal study or intuitive understanding – Kershaw succeeded to craft songs that are simultaneously immediate and intricate.

This analysis isn't meant to reduce these songs to formulae or suggest that their success can be replicated through theoretical understanding alone. What it can do is deepen our appreciation for the craft involved, showing that what might sound effortless was actually the product of serious musical knowledge applied with pop sensibility.

Before we dive into the analysis, a crucial disclaimer: it's entirely possible – even probable – that if Mr Kershaw himself were to read these theoretical explorations, he might respond with bemused surprise. "I just thought it sounded good," he might say, or "I wasn't thinking about that aspect of it at all." Artists don't always work from theoretical blueprints, and what we identify as sophisticated harmonic choices might have been intuitive decisions made in a moment of inspiration.

This gap between analytical observation and artistic intent isn't a weakness – it's actually the point. We're not attempting to read Kershaw's mind or claim special insight into his creative process. We can't know if he deliberately chose a particular chord for its unsettling qualities or simply because his fingers landed there and it felt right. What we can do is describe what's actually present in the music – what we hear when we listen carefully, and how these elements contribute to the songs' effects.

When discussing production elements, it's important to note that Kershaw's first two albums were produced by Peter Collins, whose credentials brought serious pop craftsmanship to the proceedings. Around 1979-80, Collins formed a production company with Pete Waterman (yes, the Pete Waterman later of Stock, Aitken and Waterman), who put him in charge of recording operations. Collins' early production credits included The Lambrettas' first two albums and their chart hit 'Poison Ivy.' In 1982, he scored his first number one when he co-produced Musical Youth's 'Pass the Dutchie.' Collins would go on to produce Rush, Queensrÿche, and Gary Moore, but in 1984 he was the perfect choice for Kershaw – someone who understood both pop sensibility and musical sophistication.

Let's look under the bonnet, examine the moving parts, and discover why *Human Racing* and *The Riddle* still sound so vital over forty years later.

Dancing Girls

'Dancing Girls' opens with a distinctive drum-machine rhythm – crisp, immediate, and utterly arresting – a pattern that locks the listener in before a melody even appears. The beat feels both propulsive and precise, its mechanical repetition at once synthetic and addictive. A staccato, bassy-sounding synth soon joins, its clipped phrasing adding a percussive depth to the rhythmic frame. Moments later, a higher-pitched synth line enters, gliding above with a light vibrato. Together they form a fascinating textural interplay – bright against dark, sustained against staccato – that defines the opening sound world of both song and album. The contrast between these layers feels like a dialogue between machine and melody.

Within just a few bars, Kershaw establishes not only a sound but an aesthetic. It's a masterful introduction to his debut album, instantly defining its mood and style: a world where pop gloss meets structural intelligence.

At first listen, the track feels straightforwardly upbeat. But the more you sit inside it, the more you notice a subtle sense of imbalance that serves as a vital creative tension. The rhythm section sits slightly off-centre: the bass line doesn't simply mark the beat but darts around it, often landing just before or just after where you expect. This micro-syncopation gives the groove its nervous energy. The percussion patterns are crisp and symmetrical, yet the keyboard textures shimmer in uneven layers above them, creating a controlled chaos that keeps the song perpetually in motion.

Harmonically, tension builds through subtle shifts rather than grand modulations. The chords don't always behave as expected – a turn that seems to promise brightness will suddenly darken, or vice versa. It's the musical equivalent of catching someone's expression change mid-smile. Those little harmonic feints are central to Kershaw's writing: he rarely lets a section sit comfortably in one emotional space. Instead, he tilts it, giving the listener the pleasant vertigo of something slightly unstable yet irresistibly right.

The vocal line mirrors that architecture. Kershaw's melody arcs upward in tight intervals, then leaps suddenly, like an instinct overriding calculation. You can hear how carefully it's engineered – phrases resolving at just the point of maximum tension – yet it never feels academic. His voice threads its way through a landscape of synths, a human element negotiating with the digital world around it.

After Kershaw sings the phrase "dancing girls," a brief synth interjection bursts forth – sharp, punchy, and rhythmically emphatic. It adds a spark of urgency, like a flash of light across the mix. The contrast between the smoothness of Kershaw's vocal and the suddenness of this electronic flourish captures the dynamic tension that drives the entire piece.

When the verse beginning "Soul destroyed by life's demands..." arrives, a new synth texture subtly reshapes the atmosphere. The timbre is more fluid, its tone slightly glassy, adding an extra layer of melancholy beneath the rhythmic brightness.

The instrumental section following the second chorus brings an interesting harmonic moment: a synth solo that oscillates between major and minor tonalities. This ambivalence – the shifting emotional colour between optimism and shadow – is quintessential Kershaw, amplifying the tonal tug-of-war that's been simmering beneath the song from the start and offering something more nuanced than straightforward pop euphoria.

Then, after the third chorus, another instrumental passage emerges. Over the established patterns, a high-pitched synth melody appears, its contour distinctly classical – arpeggiated, poised, and ornamented with a sense of grace. It's an exquisite detail, a fleeting echo of baroque counterpoint refracted through 1980s technology. This moment crystallises the song's duality: the ancient discipline of structure meeting the modern language of synthesizers.

The production completes the picture. Every texture has its place: bright stabs of synthesizer, a bass sound that's both rubbery and precise. The mix leaves space for the rhythm to breathe – crucial in a song that lives by its groove. The effect is paradoxical: sleek but restless, tight yet alive.

As an album opener, 'Dancing Girls' is a statement of intent. It announces Kershaw as a pop craftsman unafraid of complexity, someone who can thread sophistication through accessibility without anyone noticing the stitches. The song invites you onto the dancefloor, but beneath the movement there's an intricate architecture of harmonic sleights and rhythmic games that keep your brain as engaged as your body. That dual pleasure – the head and the feet moving together – is what would come to define Kershaw's best work.

Wouldn't It Be Good

If 'Dancing Girls' invited you into the neon-lit world of *Human Racing*, 'Wouldn't It Be Good' closes the door behind you and turns the light a cooler shade. It's a song built on contradiction – sleek on the surface, but full of ache underneath. Everything about it, from its crystalline synths to its pleading melody, seems designed to express that uneasy balance between yearning and resignation.

The song opens with that unmistakable riff – a jagged, cyclical figure played on a heavily processed guitar. Its clipped attack and metallic sheen immediately set the emotional temperature: cool, tense, a little alien. The part isn't simply an introduction; it's a character in itself, establishing the unease that will colour everything to come. The riff circles on itself like a restless thought, its harmonic shape unresolved, hinting at motion but never quite releasing. Beneath the surface polish, there's friction – the faint sense of something trying to break free from its loop. It's a perfect musical metaphor for the song's theme: people trapped in patterns of comparison and longing, always orbiting what they think they want but never arriving.

Following the opening guitar riff, a gleaming synth melody enters – confident, clear, and instantly memorable. What's striking is that this melodic figure isn't just an introductory hook or background flourish: it's the very same melody that later carries the chorus. By introducing it instrumentally first, Kershaw creates a sense of instant familiarity, as though the listener is being gently taught the tune before the words arrive. When his vocal line finally enters, it feels both fresh and inevitable – the natural next step in a musical conversation already underway.

It's a clever piece of songwriting that shows immense faith in the melody's strength. The phrasing of the synth part mirrors the shape and contour of Kershaw's vocal line so precisely that the two feel inseparable, each reinforcing the other's emotional weight. The result is cohesion and purpose: two elements serving one another, making the song deeply memorable.

The high-pitched synth comments that weave through the verses act like emotional punctuation. Each one feels like a reminder of the distance between people in the story. The mood is cold and hints at bleakness, a feeling of isolation, the precise, icy tones reflecting the emotional frost that's settled over the song's world.

Lyrically, each verse hands the story to a different person, each voice with its own shade of melancholy. What connects them all is empathy. Every speaker envies another's life, assuming that someone else's grass must be greener. Yet by structuring the song as a chain of perspectives, Kershaw quietly reveals that everyone's looking over the same fence. It's a cycle of comparison with no real escape, and the music reinforces that circular motion: progressions that seem to promise resolution but always find their way back to the same unsettled point.

What's remarkable is how the song manages to feel both bleak and warm. The bleakness comes from its architecture – the minor tonal palette, the chilly precision of the electronics, the restrained tempo that feels more like trudging than dancing. But over that framework floats Kershaw's vocal line, soft-edged and profoundly human. He doesn't belt; he *reaches*. The grain in his voice, the way he lets certain notes hover just above their pitch centres, introduces a vulnerability. The chorus, with its sighing melodic line and open vowels, allows the emotion to breathe more freely – and that contrast makes it hit harder.

The song's structure as a whole underscores this emotional geometry. The verses are tight and contained, their rhythmic grid rigid and unyielding, while the choruses open up with wider harmonies. It's as if the music itself momentarily expands to let in the human longing it's been keeping at bay. Even the guitar solo – treated, compressed, almost synthetic – feels like a cry from within. Every sonic choice contributes to that haunting sense of anguish trapped inside.

'Wouldn't It Be Good' endures because it understands something fundamental about pop emotion: that sadness and comfort can occupy the same chord, that technology can reveal rather than obscure feeling. Kershaw captures the ache of wanting another life while realising that everyone else is doing the same. It's not just a song about envy; it's a song about recognition – that moment when we see ourselves in someone else's discontent.

And that's why, over forty years on, those cold synths still cut deep. They don't chill the heart – they illuminate it.

Drum Talk

By the time 'Drum Talk' begins, *Human Racing* has already shown Kershaw's knack for introspection and polish. But this track bursts in like sunlight after the synth-lit melancholy of 'Wouldn't It Be Good.' It's exuberant, percussive, and full of colour – a celebration of rhythm itself.

At its core, 'Drum Talk' is a conversation between voice and rhythm. Kershaw uses his own vocal line as a kind of percussive instrument – not just singing *over* the groove but *inside* it. The scat-style phrases – those quick, syllabic bursts – lock perfectly with the drum sounds, turning phonetics into pure rhythm. Technology amplifies this effect: single-syllable samples of Kershaw's voice have been arranged in a lightly melodic, percussive pattern, adding texture and reinforcing the interplay between voice and drums. This approach firmly dates the track to its era, but it also contributes an inventive layer that enhances the song's rhythmic vitality. It's playful, but not throwaway: the effect is of a singer momentarily shedding the burden of words to communicate something more primal. Each nonsense syllable lands with the precision of a snare hit or tom accent, reminding us that voice and drum share the same physical heartbeat.

The rhythm section drives everything here. The groove feels part funk, part Afro-pop, part New Wave precision. The percussion has a hand-played-type looseness even as the beat sits tight within a pop framework. Over it, bright brass fanfares burst like confetti – not smooth horn-section pads, but sharp, syncopated calls that evoke street parades, festival bands, the organised chaos of a carnival. Those brass flourishes inject a world-music vibrancy, transforming the song into something that feels larger than any one genre.

Harmonically, it's relatively simple – but simplicity here is the point. The chords don't need to wander because the rhythmic motion carries the interest. You can feel the song built around the drum pattern rather than the other way around. That structure gives it a different kind of sophistication: one born of groove architecture rather than harmonic complexity.

The mix gives the percussion front-row space. The synth textures that peek through are warmer than usual, more supporting players than stars. The whole thing feels like it's breathing – a living, kinetic organism rather than a sequenced construct.

'Drum Talk' demonstrates that sophistication doesn't always mean harmonic complexity. Sometimes it means knowing when to let the rhythm speak, when to let the human voice become another drum. As Kershaw's lyrics declare, "I let the drums do the talking." It's a celebration of how sound itself can smile.

Bogart

Few pop albums of the eighties would dare to name-check Humphrey Bogart in a song title, but Kershaw's instinct is spot on. 'Bogart' isn't a novelty reference – it's a meditation on the myths we build around our heroes and the quiet ache of not quite belonging in one's own time. It's an unusually literary subject for a pop song, and Kershaw treats it with tenderness rather than irony.

The track begins with a curious, percussive sound – something metallic that immediately draws the ear. The rhythm is hypnotic but never rigid. Out of this emerges a synth riff, bright yet slightly mournful, sketching the harmonic world the song will inhabit. It's soon joined by a distorted guitar, its rough edges rubbing against the smooth synth surface. The contrast between these timbres – polished and frayed – gives the opening section remarkable textural depth. There's already rhythmic tension and emotional complexity before Kershaw has sung a word.

Texture is one of the song's most striking features. The arrangement is built from delicate, interlocking layers; nothing dominates, everything glows from within. That restraint gives the song its fragility. Even when the chorus arrives, it does so not with bombast but with a gentle widening of space, as if the soundstage itself is taking a breath.

The harmony hovers rather than settles, creating a sense of emotional suspension – a perfect match for lyrics about yearning for another era, another identity.

The progressions never shout; they sigh. Each chord feels like a half-turn of thought. Melodic lines drift upward only to fall again, as though pulled back by gravity. That push and pull gives the song its emotional depth – hope and melancholy braided so tightly you can't separate them.

In the verses, the harmonic movement feels circular and unresolved. The chords outline motion but avoid clear cadences, drifting rather than landing, which perfectly matches the song's nostalgic, dreamlike quality. The synth and guitar tones blur the harmonic edges even further, so you feel atmosphere rather than direction.

The chorus opens out a little – there's a sense of emotional expansion – but it still resists pop-style resolution. It's as though the melody wants to soar but can't quite break free. The chords feel brighter, yet they continue to float, their roots ambiguous. Even at its emotional peak, the song retains its wistful instability.

At the emotional centre is Kershaw's vocal, caught between intimacy and distance. He sings as though half inside the memory he's describing – his tone wistful, carrying a quiet desperation. There's a longing here that isn't merely nostalgic but existential. The Bogart of the title becomes less a person than an idea: a symbol of stoic glamour and moral certainty the modern world no longer seems to offer. Kershaw's narrator yearns for that clarity.

The production sustains that mood with great subtlety. The slight reverb in the chorus isn't just atmospheric;

it's structural. It creates distance, as if the song is being sung from the far end of a long corridor. Every sound seems wrapped in its own echo, suggesting the passage of time – memory refracted through nostalgia. Even the percussion – restrained, softly syncopated – feels less like a drum line than footsteps in another room.

What makes 'Bogart' so compelling is its emotional honesty. It's not a song about wanting to be a movie star; it's about wanting to matter in the way those screen icons seemed to. It's about the dissonance between how life looks and how it feels. And, in typical Kershaw fashion, that yearning is expressed through both craft and vulnerability: precise musical design carrying deeply human emotion.

The result is one of the album's most affecting moments – a pop ballad that feels like a sigh from someone out of step with their time. 'Bogart' reminds us that Kershaw wasn't just writing clever songs; he was writing emotional landscapes. Here, the landscape glows in monochrome – beautiful, lonely, and full of longing for a world that may never have existed.

Gone to Pieces

If 'Bogart' was the sigh of a dreamer, 'Gone to Pieces' is the nervous laugh that follows a breakdown. It's a brilliantly kinetic track – bright, catchy, and faintly unhinged. Beneath its polished pop surface runs a current of mania, the sound of someone trying to hold themselves together with rhythm alone.

From the first few bars, the song bounces with energy.

The bass is its heartbeat – elastic, propulsive, and endlessly inventive. It doesn't just outline the chords; it dances through them, giving the track its irresistible spring. Each note seems to lean forward into the next, as though the bass line itself is slightly anxious to keep moving. That bounce is deceptive: it feels joyful on the surface, but there's an edge to it – a sense that momentum is the only thing preventing collapse. Kershaw understood that a great pop groove can mask emotional instability, and here he builds that duality right into the bones of the song.

Lyrically, 'Gone to Pieces' deals with disintegration – not the tragic kind, but the everyday unravelling caused by pressure, expectation, and self-doubt. Yet instead of wallowing, Kershaw sets it to one of the album's most buoyant arrangements, creating that delicious contradiction that runs through so much of his work. You find yourself smiling while the song quietly falls apart.

Throughout the verse, the rhythm section functions like a coiled machine – a locked-in interplay with the bass that keeps the track oscillating between control and chaos. Layered over that engine are the remarkable high-pitched backing vocals: cartoon-like, almost manic in their pitch-bent cheerfulness. They shadow his lead line with exaggerated precision, like voices inside the narrator's head trying a little too hard to sound fine. The result is thrilling and slightly unnerving – a sonic embodiment of paranoia disguised as pop exuberance.

The production amplifies this tension beautifully. The

guitars provide percussive punctuation rather than melodic comfort; the synths that appear before the chorus sparkle like sunlight on broken glass. Every sound feels slightly heightened, as if heard through a state of nervous alertness. Even the mix is a touch claustrophobic – everything close, bright, a little too clean – perfectly mirroring the song's theme of composure under strain.

After the chorus, a burst of brass erupts into the mix, sounding halfway between fanfare and alarm. Its tonality is striking – not quite warm enough to be triumphant, not quite dissonant enough to be jarring. It occupies a tense middle ground that intensifies the song's restless momentum. The brass timbre underlines the sense of things spinning just slightly out of control – a flourish that's both exhilarating and unsettling. It's a brilliantly judged touch, heightening the track's manic brightness while hinting at the cracks beneath.

Kershaw's vocal performance is central to this balancing act. He sings with crisp precision, yet you can hear the strain beneath the surface. His phrasing darts and twists in lockstep with the rhythm, but every so often he lets a note linger too long, like a thought he can't quite suppress. That subtle instability gives the performance its humanity – the tension between composure and collapse.

'Gone to Pieces' is a masterclass in rhythmic design. The syncopation between bass and vocal, the interplay of textures, the way the groove continually resets itself – it all contributes to a kind of musical anxiety that feels propulsive rather than paralysing. It's pop as controlled chaos: every manic grin perfectly in time.

By the end, the title feels less like a lyric than a diagnosis – a summary of the song's inner state. Everything sounds intact, yet you can feel the cracks forming beneath the polish. And that's what makes 'Gone to Pieces' so compelling: in just over three minutes of dazzling rhythm and melody, it captures the sound of someone trying to stay upbeat while quietly fraying at the edges.

It's brilliant, it's catchy, and it's just a little bit mad – exactly as it should be.

Shame on You

The second side of *Human Racing* doesn't ease you back in – it jumps out of the gate. 'Shame on You' is a burst of rhythm and wit, a track that feels both effortless and meticulously built. After the emotional intricacies of the album's first half, this song resets the mood with a grin and a groove. It's pure propulsion – and it's hard to understand how it wasn't a single, because it has all the ingredients: instantly memorable hooks, danceable rhythm, and that unmistakable Kershaw blend of pop accessibility and sophistication.

From the first moment, the track radiates confidence with Kershaw's extraordinary vocal play. He uses a kind of scat-like beatboxing – a string of clipped, percussive syllables that carry rhythm and attitude. These phonemes give the song its pulse, a kind of human drum machine that feels spontaneous and playful. It's a technique you might expect from jazz or funk, but Kershaw brings it into the pop realm with precision. It's another example of his gift for blurring the boundaries between musician and arranger: the voice as instrument, texture, and rhythm section all at once.

The bass is irresistible – taut, funky, and alive with syncopation. It doesn't just sit underneath the song; it drives it, its nimble movement giving the whole piece an elastic bounce. Every line feels conversational, the kind of bass playing that talks back to the vocal rather than simply supporting it. It's the sound of an artist enjoying his groove and inviting you to join in.

The synth stabs that occur after some of the vocal phrases (for instance, "my love" and "for me" in the first verse) act like flashes of punctuation – exclamation marks in sound. They strike sharply, cutting through the groove with brilliant timing, carefully placed. Those stabs give the track a sense of momentum and surprise (especially because they're not repeated at every possible opportunity); each one lands like a spark, keeping the listener alert and the energy taut.

The chorus, though, is where 'Shame on You' really shines. It's instantly singable – compact, rhythmic, and perfectly phrased – but what makes it linger is the way Kershaw delivers it. There's something endearingly South English in his articulation of "shame on you." He doesn't smooth out the vowels like someone aiming for American radio polish; he leans into his natural accent, and in doing so, gives the phrase character. The slightly clipped consonants, the open vowel of "you," the rhythmic tilt of the phrase – it's conversational, local, human. Somehow, that simple line becomes iconic, not just because of what it says, but because of how it's said. It's the sound of pop personality unfiltered.

When the chorus returns towards the end of the song, a bright, piano-like keyboard part weaves into the texture, adding both variety and melodic lift. It's not showy – more like a subtle pattern that threads through the groove – but its effect is unmistakable. The chords – syncopated and staccato – dart in and out of the rhythm playfully. This addition gives the chorus fresh momentum, a sense of movement within repetition, and reinforces that feeling of musical conversation already at the heart of the track.

Beneath the surface charm, there's structure and sophistication at work throughout 'Shame on You.' The chord changes are tight but sly, creating small lifts of tension that make each return to the groove feel even more satisfying. The rhythm section is locked in perfect alignment, with percussion that flickers around the beat rather than sitting squarely on it – a tiny rhythmic displacement that gives the track its irresistible forward motion. The result is a song that feels both meticulously arranged and completely natural, the hallmark of Kershaw at his peak.

'Shame on You' marks the perfect opening to side two: upbeat, infectious, and bursting with musical wit. It's the sound of an artist in full control of his craft – rhythm, melody, and personality all working in harmony. Yet for all its polish, there's a warmth and humour that keeps it human. You can feel Kershaw enjoying himself, experimenting with sound, rhythm, and accent without ever losing sight of the hook.

In an album full of inventive pop moments, 'Shame on You' stands out: clever but never overbearing, funky but never forced, catchy without compromise. It's a song that struts, smiles, and grooves its way straight into memory.

Cloak and Dagger

If 'Shame on You' opens side two with sparkle and groove, 'Cloak and Dagger' follows it with shadow and suspicion. It's a song steeped in paranoia – not personal paranoia, but political. Where 'I Won't Let the Sun Go Down on Me' critiques power and brinkmanship, 'Cloak and Dagger' looks at the same world from inside the machinery: a place of secrecy, surveillance, and controlled information. It's catchy, yes, but it's the kind of catchiness that makes you uneasy even as you tap your foot. The track's opening immediately sets a mood of watchfulness. The groove is tight and insistent, pulsing with the kind of rhythmic discipline that mirrors its subject matter – order hiding chaos.

In the verse, Kershaw builds tension not just through words but through the dialogue between his voice and the instrumentation. For instance, following the phrases "along the corridors of power" and "what it's got to say," there's a low, bassy response – slightly different in timbre each time, but both sounding almost like an afterthought whispered by the system he's describing. These musical comments sit in a dark register, close to the floor of the mix, and move in short, deliberate phrases. The melody they trace isn't linear or reassuring; it dips and twists, shadowing the vocal but never quite resolving. This interaction creates a sense of call and response between man and machine – between the singer and the unseen forces he's warning about.

Harmonically, the verse operates in a minor tonal space, its chords shifting in half-light – neither fully stable nor dramatically dissonant. That harmonic uncertainty mirrors the song's themes of secrecy and surveillance: you're never quite sure what key you're standing in. Kershaw's vocal delivery amplifies this mood beautifully. He sings low and tight, his phrasing clipped, his tone restrained as though cautious of being overheard. There's tension in the quiet – the kind that suggests someone listening on the other end of the line.

The section that begins "We know what you're doing..." functions as both lyrics and a rhythmic motif, acting almost like a drum fill. Each statement snaps the listener back into the groove, punctuating the song with a kind of bureaucratic menace. It's brilliantly economical writing: simple lines that carry equal weight as commentary and percussive propulsion.

The chorus arrives like a burst of light through a locked room. Kershaw uses contrast as his chief weapon here. After the clipped restraint of the verse, the chorus expands – both sonically and emotionally. The synth stabs and distorted bass leading into it create a sudden drop in depth, a widening of the sound field that makes the hook hit twice as hard. And then, soaring above that density, come those higher-pitched melodic synth phrases that follow the lines "Our future in their hands" and "Our world behind closed doors." They shimmer like brief flashes of transparency in a song otherwise cloaked in opacity – the perfect sonic reflection of the lyrics' theme: what's hidden, what leaks out, what we're allowed to see.

Kershaw's vocal performance is a study in range and control. The phrase "Cloak and Dagger" is delivered low in his register, almost muttered, with a dark texture that feels conspiratorial – the sound of someone leaning in to share a secret. In contrast, when he sings "Our future in their hands" and "Our world behind closed doors," his voice opens upward, the vowels stretching into a kind of exasperated cry. That climb in register doesn't just show off his range; it dramatises the song's emotional arc – the shift from secrecy to exposure, from control to revelation.

The guitar solo is another masterstroke. It's lean, expressive, and slightly rough-edged, cutting through the smooth electronic textures like something human breaking into a digital world. Kershaw doesn't go for flash; he chooses phrasing and tone that serve the song's sense of tension. The solo feels like a voice – a reflective one trying to express what can't quite be said in the lyrical sections, a brief surge of emotion in a world otherwise ruled by restraint.

The arrangement throughout is intricate but never fussy. The bass has a slight grit to it, distorted just enough to create friction against the gleaming synths. Percussive elements work in tandem to maintain the pulse – crisp, clipped, always pushing forward. Every sound seems placed with purpose, as though the song itself were under surveillance, nothing left to chance. Yet within that precision there's energy, even rebellion. The groove refuses to sit still; it keeps pressing, shifting, insinuating movement within confinement.

Lyrically, 'Cloak and Dagger' feels like a companion piece to 'I Won't Let the Sun Go Down on Me.' Both look at systems of control and the psychological toll of living beneath them. But with 'Cloak and Dagger' you don't just hear the paranoia; you *feel* it in the rhythm, in the clipped delivery, in the alternating light and shadow of its arrangement.

'Cloak and Dagger' proves once again that Kershaw could make sophisticated pop without sacrificing immediacy. It's funky, it's political, it's unsettling – and, like so much of his best work, it hides complexity in plain sight.

Faces

By the time 'Faces' arrives, side two of *Human Racing* has already delivered brightness ('Shame on You') and tension ('Cloak and Dagger'). 'Faces' shifts the emotional temperature again – inward, reflective, and quietly haunted.

The song begins in a kind of drifting reverie. The verse feels meandering, harmonically uncertain, as if the music itself is searching for direction. The chords move with a curious restlessness, never quite resolving. The rhythm section holds back, offering only a light pulse beneath the synth wash, while the melody traces long, questioning lines that seem to wander rather than arrive. Listening to it, you get the sense of thought turning over in real time: an interior monologue set to music.

Then, suddenly, the chorus bursts open. The drums snap into focus, the rhythm tightens, and the song transforms into something almost militant – a march of conviction after the drift of doubt. The melodic element, which has floated weightlessly through the verse, now comes to the forefront, demanding and memorable. The bass locks in with a muscular insistence. It's as though the song has remembered its purpose and stood to attention. That contrast – between the searching verses and the regimented chorus – gives 'Faces' its emotional impact. You can feel the internal struggle between faith and uncertainty, reflection and resolution.

Kershaw's use of vocals is particularly powerful. In the verses, he sings quietly, introspectively, but when the chorus hits, his delivery opens into something firmer, almost defiant. That movement from introspection to declaration mirrors the song's structure perfectly.

In the verses, the guitar provides texture rather than lead, its clean, reverb-laced tones glinting between the beats. In the chorus, however, the sound fills out – fuller, more assertive – complementing the marching rhythm in a way that sounds almost percussive. You can hear the studio craftsmanship at work: every part serving the emotional narrative rather than drawing attention to itself.

After the line "Yes, I realised the voice was me," a new synth idea emerges, quietly at first, but instantly transformative. It's a glassy, ascending pattern – bright yet brittle – that seems to shimmer just out of reach. Its tonality is ambiguous: major enough to suggest hope, but coloured with tensions that never quite resolve. It doesn't anchor the harmony so much as illuminate it from a different angle, creating the sense of a revelation that's not entirely comfortable. With it, Kershaw's voice ("Just when you really think you're going places...") carries more urgency now – his tone sharper, the phrasing taut – as if he's stepped out of the reflective haze of the earlier verses and into confrontation with what he's found. The synth's clarity feels almost interrogative, a light held up to the self.

Then comes one of the song's most striking moments. The chorus returns but the instruments drop away, leaving only Kershaw's voice surrounded by layered, reverbed female backing vocals and the lightest of bass as a background texture. The sound is suddenly cavernous, almost sacred, yet something about it feels off-kilter. The harmonies bloom like a choir, but there's an unease in their perfection – a suggestion of ritual rather than release. It's beautiful and faintly chilling, like faith rendered mechanical. That choral quality amplifies the song's spiritual tension: devotion and doubt co-existing in the same echo.

When the full arrangement returns, the effect is like a surge of clarity after a moment of stillness. The rhythm locks back into place, the guitar and drums reassert their structure, and the chorus once again marches forward with renewed conviction. But the emotional equilibrium never quite returns.

As the song draws to a close, the ending lingers. The final syllable – "war" – is stretched and sustained, its sound gradually detaching from the human voice into something processed, almost spectral. It's as though technology takes over where Kershaw's voice leaves, the machine holding the note. That sustained sound hovers in the air, unresolved and ghostly, before finally descending in a slow pitch bend that feels more like surrender than closure. It's an ending that leaves the listener suspended – moved, unsettled, and quietly haunted.

Lyrically, the song carries an unmistakable weight, even if its meaning remains blurred. In a late-nineties interview, Kershaw admitted he couldn't quite remember what 'Faces' was about, though he suspected it dealt with "the hypocrisy of some organised religions." That forgetfulness feels almost poetic, because the song itself sounds like an act of remembering – or trying to. The sense of searching, of reaching for something half-remembered and half-lost, runs through every bar.

The music mirrors that idea: the meandering verses as spiritual questioning, the chorus as a moment of dogmatic certainty. And yet even in that militaristic confidence, something fragile remains. The melody strains upward as though unsure whether to shout or pray.

'Faces' doesn't resolve; it reflects, and that's what makes

it so powerful. You can sense a young songwriter wrestling not just with structure and sound, but with meaning itself – and that tension between faith, doubt, and craft is what gives 'Faces' its haunting staying power.

I Won't Let the Sun Go Down on Me

'I Won't Let the Sun Go Down on Me' bursts open into something that feels like light itself. The track begins with a brilliant, buoyant synth melody: a motif so bright and inviting it could almost soundtrack a children's television show. Its tone is clear, sparkling, and optimistic, built from upward intervals that seem to rise towards the sky. The music beams with optimism, even though the lyrics to follow speak of fear, frustration, and nuclear dread.

After the song's initial opening hook, there's a short instrumental passage that feels like a held breath before the verse begins. The rhythm tightens and the synths pulse in short, clipped figures, as though gathering themselves for the song's first statement. It's a moment of suspension – the optimism of the introduction held in check, waiting to see what form it will take. That sense of anticipation primes the listener perfectly: the groove is about to land, but the tension in those few bars makes its arrival all the more satisfying.

When the verse kicks in – "Forty winks in the lobby" – the rhythm snaps immediately into a tight, danceable groove. The percussion has that early-eighties precision: drum machine crispness softened by a sense of swing. The bass moves with a springy, almost elastic quality, keeping the track buoyant rather than mechanical. It's pop built for movement – hips, feet, and shoulders – and yet, tucked inside that rhythmic joy is a kind of tension. What's fascinating is how happy the song sounds overall. The verses shimmer with major-key brightness.

After the lyric "plastic smiles," a distorted guitar line cuts through the mix like a sudden flash of grit on an otherwise polished surface. Its tone is dry and mid-heavy, sitting slightly outside the synthetic sheen of the arrangement, which gives it a jarring, grinding edge. It's not there for heroics; it's punctuation – a raised eyebrow in musical form. That brief, rough gesture breaks the song's smoothness just enough to remind you that all this brightness has bite.

In the section beginning "Good or bad, like it or not..." the track pivots both harmonically and emotionally. The chords shift into a tighter loop, the synths thinning slightly to leave more space for the vocals. Kershaw's phrasing becomes more declarative, and the melody pushes insistently upward. The propulsion here comes not from volume or tempo but from conviction: every line feels like it's being pushed against resistance.

The chorus soars with an almost evangelical lift. That hook – "I won't let the sun go down on me" – is so melodic and affirmative that it's easy to mistake for something bordering on spiritual. In truth, it's closer to an anti-apocalypse anthem, a protest against resignation in the face of nuclear anxiety. In the context of 1983-84, that fear was everywhere: missile crises, protest marches, 'Protect and Survive.' But Kershaw disguises it in melody, transforming dread into defiance. The chorus doesn't sound like denial – it sounds like determination. The refusal to "let the sun go down" becomes both literal and symbolic: an insistence on life, light, and human endurance.

The track's replay value lies in contradiction. It's irresistibly danceable – bright synths, bouncing rhythmic bass, tight vocal phrasing – yet every listen reveals something bittersweet underneath. The instrumental arrangement is a masterclass in pop layering: those shimmering synths that glint like sunlight on water; the bass line that skips and ducks beneath the beat; the subtle harmonies that widen the chorus without overwhelming it.

In the verses, Kershaw's vocal delivery is brisk and rhythmically precise – he almost percusses his words, which gives the lyrics a conversational urgency. In the chorus, the backing vocals echo and extend the main melody, adding a communal feel: not just one person's declaration, but a collective human cry. When the chorus returns again and again, it doesn't wear out – it builds momentum. Each repetition feels like another refusal to surrender. That's what gives the track such longevity; it feels inexhaustible.

The song is one of Kershaw's best examples of how rhythm and melody can work together to create joy even in tension. The syncopated pulse of the verse keeps you slightly off balance, while the even, open phrasing of the chorus resolves that feeling with clarity. You could dance to it endlessly without ever feeling it drag. It's perfectly structured pop – concise, balanced, and endlessly listenable.

Even now, decades later, it's easy to hear why 'I Won't Let the Sun Go Down on Me' became one of Kershaw's most enduring songs. Its positivity isn't naive; it's deliberate – a kind of musical resistance. He takes one of the darkest subjects of his time and wraps it in melody so luminous that listeners can't help but smile. It's pop alchemy: fear turned into something that makes you move, maybe even hope.

Human Racing

The album closes with its title track – slow-moving, reflective, and quietly profound. After the brightness and rhythmic drive of 'I Won't Let the Sun Go Down on Me,' 'Human Racing' feels like a long exhale, a moment to stand still and look around. It opens with drums that are spacious and deliberate – not propulsive, but atmospheric, each hit separated by air and echo. The gentle synth line is unhurried, almost meditative, giving space for every melodic idea to unfold at its own pace. The result is a sense of suspension, as though time itself has slowed down to let the song think.

Musically, it's one of Kershaw's most delicate constructions. Beneath the calm surface lies intricate layering – a soft interplay of synth, bass, and subtle melodic threads that weave in and out without ever dominating. The bass moves gently, almost conversationally, outlining harmonies with restraint rather than insistence. Every element has room to breathe. This sense of space allows the listener to focus on the subtleties – the way a note lingers just a fraction longer than expected, the faint shimmer of keyboard textures that seem to glimmer and fade like memories.

Kershaw's vocal performance is tender, wistful, and slightly detached – not cold, but introspective. There's a hint of whimsy in his phrasing, a lightness that keeps the melancholy from becoming heavy. You can hear it in the way he stretches syllables, in the soft upward turns at the ends of phrases, as if he's constantly questioning rather than declaring. His tone conveys both longing and understanding, the feeling of someone observing humanity from a distance – sympathetic, bemused, a little heartbroken.

The melody itself is full of quiet delights. It doesn't reach for grand hooks or sharp contours; instead, it moves with conversational grace, unfolding like thought put to song. Yet there's always a pull – a gentle lift in the melodic line that carries the listener upward just before falling back into repose. This push and pull, hope and resignation, gives the song its emotional texture. You feel both the fragility and the persistence of the human condition it describes.

Lyrically, 'Human Racing' seems to reflect on the absurdity and beauty of modern existence – people rushing, competing, striving without always knowing why. There's empathy in the observation: Kershaw doesn't judge; he simply notes the chaos and contradiction of being alive. The title phrase captures that double meaning perfectly – the "race" we're all running, and the species running it. The song's leisurely pace feels almost like an antidote to that race – a reminder to slow down, to listen, to think.

What makes the track especially affecting is its balance between melancholy and wonder. The synths shimmer like distant stars, creating an otherworldly calm, while the melody hums with human warmth. The contrast between the machine-like precision of the electronic arrangement and the softness of Kershaw's vocal delivery encapsulates one of his greatest gifts as a songwriter: turning technology into emotion. You can hear the human heart beating quietly inside the circuitry.

As the song drifts towards its close, it fades not with finality but with continuation, as if the reflection could go on forever. It's a deeply fitting end to the album, summarising everything *Human Racing* has explored: ambition, anxiety, connection, isolation, and the longing to make sense of it all.

'Human Racing' is more than a closing track – it's the album's mirror, showing us what's left after all the running and noise. In its gentle pulse and melodic introspection, you can hear the sound of Kershaw's artistic integrity: thoughtfulness disguised as pop, complexity cloaked in simplicity, emotion carried by restraint. It's the kind of song that doesn't need to work hard for our attention – it just understands.

Don Quixote

The Riddle begins with a burst of colour and rhythm that feels both worldly and whimsical. 'Don Quixote' is a song alive with movement – a kinetic, melodic festivity that immediately commands attention. It's no coincidence that this is a track born from melody before meaning. Kershaw has said that he wrote the tune first, walking around the house singing nonsense syllables – "gor-gon-zola" – until inspiration struck. The wordplay eventually found its form in "Don Quixote," but the melodic DNA was already there: lilting, energetic, and unmistakably Mediterranean in flavour.

That sense of Spanish influence is woven deep into the composition. The rhythm has a subtle samba feel – syncopated, sunlit, full of motion – while the melodic contours lean towards the exotic, with phrases that dance around the tonic before resolving downward like a flourish of flamenco guitar. Even without a single castanet, you can hear Spain in the bones of the track: the percussive drive, the way the chords move with a kind of rolling gait, like the rhythmic trot of Quixote's horse itself.

From its opening bars, the song radiates energy. The percussion is bright and restless – tight, crisp, and with accents that add sparkle. The bass line bounces with playful precision, anchoring the groove while giving the whole thing a buoyant, danceable pulse. Over this, a short synth line builds anticipation with its ascending patterns, punching through in rhythmic stabs that provide both melody and momentum. The brass melody that follows lends a kind of theatrical grandeur to the track, evoking a procession or parade. They're "brass" not of an orchestra, but of imagination: heroic, cartoonish, larger than life. It's a perfect match for the song's subject – a dreamer shouting at windmills, both ridiculous and noble.

The verse flows effortlessly, Kershaw's vocal line winding around the syncopated rhythm like ribbons in motion. There's an elasticity to the phrasing; the words seem to ride the groove rather than sit squarely on it. Then, when he reaches the urgent passage – "Superman, Lois Lane..." – the whole song tightens. The tempo doesn't change, but the rhythmic phrasing becomes clipped, almost breathless, mirroring the lyrical rush of modern references tumbling over one another. It's a brilliant shift in energy: the listener goes from swaying to leaning forward, carried by momentum. Kershaw understood how to build contrast within a pop song – how to give it narrative shape through rhythm and melody alone.

There's a playful complexity to the song's harmonic movement. The chords don't simply loop; they wander, hinting at modulations and unexpected turns that keep the ear engaged. It's another sign of Kershaw's compositional intelligence – the way he folds sophistication into accessibility. The listener might not notice the shifting tonalities consciously, but they feel the freshness in every turn.

'Don Quixote' bursts with personality. It's bright, restless, rhythmically intricate, and melodically generous – a perfect album opener that declares *The Riddle* as a record of global textures and conceptual breadth. The fusion of samba rhythm, pop form, and literary inspiration feels effortlessly natural here. It's the sound of an artist expanding his palette – reaching outward while still sounding unmistakably himself.

Kershaw's Quixote isn't a tragic figure; he's a pop hero – flawed, funny, determined, dancing towards an ideal. And in that dance – in those clever rhythms, those shining brass fanfares, that melody born from "gorgonzola" nonsense – you hear the joy of creation itself.

Know How

If 'Don Quixote' opened *The Riddle* with flamboyant rhythm and imagination, 'Know How' follows it with something tighter, funkier, and more grounded. Where the first track galloped through Spain, this one struts through the barracks – all clipped precision, marching rhythm, and sly satire. It's a masterclass in pop groove and tonal character, marrying sharp social observation with infectious rhythmic arrangements.

The song bursts to life on a wave of rhythmic confidence: that taut, syncopated bass line locked perfectly to the snappy drum pattern. There's real bounce here – a rubber-band elasticity that drives the track forward without ever losing its composure. The funk influence is unmistakable, yet this isn't imitation of American R&B; it's funk filtered through an English pop sensibility, crisp and clever rather than loose and meandering. Every note in that bass line feels deliberate, giving the song a pulse that's both danceable and slightly militaristic. It's as if discipline and groove are shaking hands.

Over the rhythm bed, bright, percussive synth textures jab in short bursts, accenting the downbeats and punctuating Kershaw's vocal line. The verses, sung with a clipped precision that mirrors the lyrical content – a self-important authority figure bragging about rank and order – glide along this funk framework with effortless propulsion. You can practically see the strut in the performance.

After the line "with one shake of the head," the funk tightens for the chorus, then a shimmering synth line spirals upward – melodic, airy, and just slightly whimsical. It's a flash of colour against the disciplined rhythm, as though imagination were momentarily breaking through the rigidity the lyrics describe. This contrast – melody blooming out of structure – gives the song its charm and sophistication.

On the spoken section – a half-comic, half-menacing interlude of "I don't care who you say you are, I can't let you in here" – the delivery has the officious chill of a security guard, and what follows is one of the track's great surprises. Instead of returning to the expected verse or chorus, the song takes a left turn – melodically and harmonically unexpected; synth chords climbing upward into a new key area that brightens the whole texture. For a few bars, the song seems to transcend its own structure, opening into something almost cinematic, before snapping back into the tight, funky grid that began it. That moment of surprise is pure Kershaw: musically intelligent but emotionally intuitive, giving the listener something they didn't know they wanted until it happens.

The arrangement is a marvel of stylistic diversity. Beneath the funk lies a pulse that occasionally slips into march-like territory – the rhythmic discipline giving it a sense of order. Yet the synth embellishments, playful melodic fragments, and shifting harmonic colours add movement and wit. There's a kind of satirical elegance to it all, as if Kershaw were scoring a bureaucratic parade.

His vocal performance walks a fine line between character and clarity. He delivers the verses with an almost spoken precision – clipped consonants, short phrases – embodying the officious narrator, while his tone softens and widens in the chorus. That subtle shift in timbre helps the song breathe: authority turning into rhythm, rigidity into art.

The production, too, is pristine. Each instrument occupies its own space: the bass warm and rounded, the drums snappy but not brittle, the synths bright without crowding the mix. There's an architectural quality to it – you can hear the design in the air between the parts.

Ultimately, 'Know How' is a rhythmically accomplished piece. It grooves, it struts, and it sparkles – yet beneath that infectious surface lies commentary on control, hierarchy, and the human tendency to hide behind rules. You can dance to it without catching any of that, of course – and maybe that's the point. The groove seduces first, and the meaning comes later.

It's the sound of confidence: a songwriter who truly does know how.

You Might

The third track of *The Riddle* begins with a jolt of energy – a distorted guitar figure that hints at something closer to rock than pop. For a brief moment, you expect the song to roar to life in a blaze of guitars. But then Kershaw pulls the rug out. An icy synth slides in over the top, cool and glassy, redirecting the track into a more atmospheric, almost cinematic space. That opening instant – a clash of warmth and chill, muscle and mist – perfectly encapsulates what makes 'You Might' so compelling. Within seconds, Kershaw creates drive, urgency, and emotional contrast, all before the first line is sung.

The momentum never lets up. The drums lock into a tight 4/4, propelled by a snare-type sound that snaps on the second and fourth beats – the unmistakable hallmark of 1980s pop production. But where some tracks of the era use that backbeat for sheer gloss, Kershaw uses it for tension. The crispness of the rhythm keeps the song's dreamier harmonies from drifting away. It's that contrast – mechanical pulse meeting emotional melody – that gives the song its bite. You can dance to it, but there's something in the rhythm that feels like it's pushing you forward, urging you to go somewhere.

Above that rhythmic foundation, the verse unfolds with surprising tenderness. There's a sentimentality to the melody – not sugary or nostalgic, but quietly yearning. The vocal line glides across chord changes that tug just slightly against expectation, creating moments of gentle ache. Harmonically, Kershaw weaves between major and minor inflections in a way that evokes hope and doubt in the same breath.

When the chorus arrives – "You might be an oil tycoon. You might be a Cobb cartoon..." – it's playful in language but deadly serious in tone, the arrangement driving forward with a determination that underlines the irony of the lyrics. The second and fourth beats continue to hit hard here, giving the chorus its forward thrust and danceable snap. It's pure eighties in construction, but sophisticated in its emotional execution – polished enough for radio, layered enough for repeat listening.

Then there's that wonderful vocal moment in the second verse – the melisma on "hero" in the line "You could've been a hero." It's one of those small, expressive touches that reveal Kershaw's instinct for melody. Rather than singing the word straight, he lets it ripple upward, stretching the syllable like a wistful thought. It's not showy; it's emotional. The flourish turns the line from statement to lament – the sound of possibility slipping away.

Instrumentally, the track is rich without being cluttered. The bass moves with a lively spring, often syncopating against the steady drums to create a sense of push and pull. The guitar, introduced so assertively at the start, settles into the texture as the song progresses, occasionally resurfacing with clean, echoing chords that add shimmer to the mix. The synths are the real scene-setters, though – those cool, glassy tones that dart and swell, giving the track a distinctive emotional temperature.

There's a bridge that feels like both release and revelation. The repeated "You are what you are" feels like a small moment of truth amid the song's irony. A flash of acceptance – possibly painful to admit – in a piece otherwise focused on unfulfilled potential.

Stylistically, 'You Might' is deceptively diverse. It borrows from rock in its guitar tone and rhythmic insistence, from synth-pop in its electronic texture. Yet it never feels patchwork – Kershaw fuses those elements into something distinctly his own. The result is a track that brims with confidence and musical intelligence.

And yes, it could easily have been a single. It's got everything: immediacy, groove, memorable hooks, emotional resonance. But more than that, it showcases Kershaw's instinct for balance – between warmth and coolness, irony and sincerity, pop accessibility and compositional depth.

By the time 'You Might' ends, you've been taken through an entire emotional arc: the promise of something powerful, the coolness of reflection, the melancholy of what could have been. It's the sound of eighties pop at its best – smart, stylish, and full of heart.

Wild Horses

'Wild Horses' opens with an easy, swaying groove that immediately feels different from anything that's come before it on *The Riddle*. There's a faint reggae inflection in the rhythm – a gentle off-beat lilt that gives the track a kind of relaxed, sun-dappled motion. Yet, in true

Kershaw fashion, the influence is more suggestion than imitation. The rhythm feels light on its feet, but the harmonies and synth textures that hover above it place the song firmly in his distinct musical world.

At the centre of it all is that mellow synth riff – smooth, unhurried, quietly hypnotic. It doesn't shout for attention, but it sets the tone completely. The sound is warm but slightly glassy, the sort of tone that seems to hang in mid-air rather than sit in the mix. It creates a sense of calm distance – a perfect foil for the subtle rhythmic movement beneath. That mixture of steadiness and shimmer gives 'Wild Horses' its particular emotional colour: wistful, thoughtful, quietly assured.

The percussion palette is one of the song's secret strengths. You can hear a wide range of sounds – not just the usual drum kit, but percussive textures that feel almost organic, like pipe drums or hand-tapped surfaces. There's air and space between each element, making the rhythm section feel expansive and three-dimensional. The result is that the track never feels static. Even in its most reflective moments, there's movement and life within the rhythm, a sense of gentle sway that keeps the listener engaged.

When the second verse arrives – "On the side of a mountain..." – something subtly shifts. A new synth melody enters, weaving softly over the top of the arrangement. It's a small change, but it transforms the atmosphere. The first verse felt earthbound, grounded in its rhythm and texture. The second feels as if it's opening upward – a breath of cold air over the mountain scene being described. That melodic layer adds a shimmer of otherworldliness, as though the song has suddenly lifted its eyes from the everyday to something larger and more contemplative.

Then comes one of those moments Kershaw does so well – the delicate vocal melisma on the word "to" in "no one to do it to." It's just a few notes, but it's so gracefully executed that it catches the ear instantly. There's a little ache in it, a quiet human moment amid the technical precision of the production. It's these touches that make his singing so distinctive: controlled but expressive, thoughtful but never detached.

The following chorus subtly changes its clothes – the percussion pattern shifts, opening up new syncopations that refresh the song's momentum. It's one of several places where Kershaw refuses to let repetition breed complacency. Each chorus feels familiar but newly detailed, as if the song is evolving as it goes. This constant variation within a conventional pop structure is part of his genius: he keeps the listener's ear alive without ever breaking the flow.

Near the song's end, a short guitar solo slips into the mix – not flashy or indulgent, but melodic and poised. It's followed by the chorus returning in a new key, lifting the whole emotional temperature. That modulation is subtle but satisfying; it feels like a window opening, letting in a burst of light. The brassy-sounding synth interjections amplify that effect. They're bright and triumphant, cutting through the mix with an almost celebratory energy. By this point, the song has blossomed from its laid-back beginnings into something surprisingly expansive, a miniature journey of its own.

Lyrically, 'Wild Horses' mirrors some of the ideas from 'Wouldn't It Be Good.' Where that earlier song dealt with envy and comparison – the grass always greener elsewhere – this one looks outward and says, in effect, 'I wouldn't trade places.' The two characters Kershaw sketches – the corporate man and the man of nature – both seem trapped in their own lives. The refrain "Wild horses wouldn't drag me there" becomes a declaration of self-awareness: contentment not born of comfort, but of knowing where one belongs. Whether Kershaw meant the parallel or stumbled into it instinctively, the thematic connection deepens both songs when heard side by side.

As a piece of pop craftsmanship, 'Wild Horses' is masterful. It's a track of quiet variety – every verse, every chorus, every instrumental touch introducing something new. Yet it never feels busy or cluttered. Everything breathes. The production is clean but human, the playing disciplined but warm. Like so many of Kershaw's finest songs, it could easily have been a single – memorable, stylish, and full of understated intelligence.

By the time it ends, you're left with the feeling of having been taken somewhere – from the top of an office block to the side of a mountain, and finally to a place of acceptance. 'Wild Horses' is one of those deceptively simple songs that unfolds more meaning the more you listen. It's mellow, rhythmic, and quietly profound.

Easy

'Easy' is one of those tracks that makes you sit up a little straighter the moment it begins. The intro alone – a spiky, syncopated funk-guitar riff – feels like it's wandered in from a different record entirely. There's a tight, jazzy line whose chromatic twists immediately catch the ear. The notes slide and hop in unexpected places, outlining chords that sound more like jazz than pop. It's a bold, brilliant way to begin, instantly throwing the listener off balance and signalling that this isn't just another pop tune.

Once the groove settles, the catchiness remains in full force. The verse rides on that buoyant funk rhythm – springy bass, clipped guitar, drums locked in with a light but precise articulation. The melody flows naturally over the top, and Kershaw's dynamic vocal delivery makes the technical complexity feel effortless.

Then comes the chorus, and it's irresistible. "Easy we come, easy we go" might sound simple on paper, but in Kershaw's hands it's both hooky and subtly complex. The phrasing sits just ahead of the beat, giving it a gentle push, and the harmonies underneath shift in quietly surprising ways. It's the kind of chorus that sticks – bright, memorable, perfectly balanced between intellect and instinct. It's easy to imagine the song as a single; had MCA been willing to take a small risk on something funkier and more jazz-coloured, it might have found an eager audience beyond Kershaw's core fans.

In many ways, 'Easy' harks back to his pre-solo days in

the band Fusion. The jazz and funk influences that shaped that group's 1980 album are clearly alive here – the tight interplay between bass and drums, the chord voicings that sneak in a little harmonic colour, the rhythmic precision that feels more like a player's creativity than a producer's trick. It's a song that reminds you Kershaw wasn't just a songwriter with a good ear for melody, but a serious musician who could sit comfortably in a groove-based ensemble.

Before the verse that begins "Wake me up, I'm fast asleep," Kershaw drops in a moment of scat-style vocalising – playful, rhythmic syllables that blur the line between percussion and melody. It's a charming nod to jazz phrasing, and, with the addition of harmonised backing vocals, it adds a human, improvisatory quality to a track that's otherwise meticulously arranged. This section bridges beautifully into the new verse, giving the song a touch of spontaneity that offsets its studio polish.

The line "And a temporary plan" gets a subtle but striking vocal treatment – a slight effect on the voice that catches the ear and injects a spark of variety into the verse. It's a small production flourish used sparingly but effectively: just enough to keep the texture fresh without distracting from the song itself.

As the track progresses towards its finale, a new melodic idea appears – a synth line that plays a bright, ascending figure over the existing groove. It's a moment of tonal contrast: after so much jazz-inflected harmony, this new melody feels cleaner, more pop-oriented, almost like a beam of sunlight breaking through the clouds. It slots in perfectly with the rest of the arrangement, adding another layer of energy without crowding the mix. The way it interacts with the bass and drums – weaving between them but never overpowering – is a quiet testament to the song's balance.

Throughout 'Easy,' there's a sense of controlled looseness. The playing is tight but never stiff, the harmonies adventurous but always melodic. Even the lyrical refrain – "Easy we come, easy we go" – feels like a kind of philosophy for the song itself: breezy, clever, deceptively relaxed.

As a side-closer, it's inspired. After the thematic and stylistic variety of side one, 'Easy' feels like a deep breath before the album flips over – a reminder that Kershaw could pivot from pop precision to jazz-funk sophistication without losing his identity for a second. It's slyly technical, effortlessly groovy, and just plain fun to listen to.

If 'Easy' had been released as a single, it might have surprised people – not least because it shows just how far beyond the pop label Kershaw's musical vocabulary really extended. It's the sound of a songwriter stretching out, testing his own limits, and doing it with a grin.

The Riddle

'The Riddle' isn't just the title track of Nik Kershaw's second album; it's arguably one of his most iconic compositions. It's the kind of song that perfectly distils his peculiar genius: musically intricate, emotionally resonant, and melodically unforgettable – all while in many ways being utterly unclassifiable.

'The Riddle' begins not with synth sparkle or pop bombast, but with the rattle of military-style drumming. It's an arresting opening – disciplined, deliberate, and instantly unusual for a chart single. Right from the first bar, it establishes a sense of formality and ritual. These aren't dance drums; they're drums of procession, of purpose. It's as if the song is preparing to march rather than to groove. That small choice sets 'The Riddle' apart before the melody even begins.

Then comes the guitar riff – one of the most haunting and beautiful in 1980s pop. Its shape is unexpected: a melody that seems to wander and yet land perfectly every time. It's not just catchy; it's curious. The notes move in ways that feel simultaneously logical and dreamlike, touching on melancholy and wonder in equal measure. That's the magic of it – the hook is so strong it could loop forever, and yet it carries emotional weight. You can hum it, but you also feel it.

Harmonically, that riff hints at modal colours – not quite major, not quite minor, more like something from folk or early classical music. This tonal ambiguity gives the melody its wistfulness. Each return to that phrase feels like a question asked again and again, never quite answered – fitting, perhaps, for a song whose lyrics were eventually revealed to be nonsensical placeholders. The guitar's bright tone offsets the melancholy, giving the phrase both sadness and light.

The synth line that accompanies the riff is equally striking – a weaving, almost Baroque harpsichord figure that seems to thread its way through the arrangement. It's elegant and agile, a little flourish of classical counterpoint tucked into a pop framework. This motif returns at key moments, like a decorative seam running through the song's fabric. Every time it reappears, it deepens the sense of enchantment, as if the piece were looping through a riddle of its own.

When the verse arrives, it flows naturally from the introduction – the rhythm steady, the melody winding through unusual contours that feel folk-inspired. There's something pastoral about it, something rooted in English melodic tradition. And yet it never feels quaint or nostalgic. The overall production, with its clean synths and layered harmonies, keeps the sound vividly modern. It's this combination – ancient-sounding melody dressed in futuristic textures – that makes 'The Riddle' so fascinating.

The genius of 'The Riddle' reveals itself fully when the chorus arrives – it's built on the exact same melodic phrase as that haunting guitar riff from the introduction. This isn't laziness or lack of ideas; it's compositional brilliance. That melody proves so robust, so perfectly crafted, that it works equally well as an instrumental hook and as a vehicle for vocals. It's like a piece of architecture so well-designed it functions perfectly as both foundation and façade. The melody has such intrinsic strength that it can carry the weight of being both the song's calling card and its emotional centre. "Near a tree by a river..." essentially sings the guitar riff back to itself, creating a satisfying unity between the instrumental and vocal elements.

The section beginning "I got time to kill..." brings a fresh burst of melodic invention. The chords shift subtly, opening up a new emotional space – more expansive, almost wistful. It's as if the song is pausing to breathe, the listener caught between motion and reflection. The Baroque-style harpsichord-type line comes to the fore in this section – its bright, intricate motion lending the moment a unique and curious quality, part elegance, part enigma. Kershaw's voice, expressive but restrained, gives the melody an aching clarity that makes even nonsense lyrics sound profound.

After "Wise men's child" the music turns back on itself – the military-type theme returns, fuller in texture but complete with the same rhythmic insistence that opened the track. This time, the drums are joined by whistling – a simple, almost rustic whistle that carries the chorus melody. The effect is magical. The formal precision of the drumming meets the informal, human warmth of the whistle, creating a juxtaposition that feels both symbolic and deeply satisfying. It's the meeting of duty and daydream, discipline and freedom – a sound image of pride, purpose, and perseverance, like how soldiers might whistle while marching.

Few pop songs manage this blend of textures so seamlessly. The military-style percussion suggests resolve, while the folk-like melody embodies yearning. Together, they create an emotional world that feels strangely timeless, as if this could be a marching song from an imaginary past. That it also works as a sleek 1980s pop single is nothing short of miraculous.

And of course, the irony is that its lyrics – initially the subject of fan over-analysis – mean nothing at all. They were, as Kershaw has admitted, placeholders that stuck. Yet perhaps that's part of the song's allure. Stripped of specific meaning, the music itself becomes the message. The melody, the rhythm, the tone – these carry all the emotion and mystery that the words only gesture towards. 'The Riddle' is less a puzzle to be solved than a feeling to inhabit – one of curiosity, melancholy, and quiet determination.

It's a track that shouldn't work on paper – military-style percussion, folk-like melody, Baroque-inspired synths – yet it does, spectacularly. This is Kershaw at his most fearless: writing pop music that feels both personal and mythic, complex and completely accessible. The result is not just one of his greatest songs, but one of the most distinctive pop recordings of the 1980s – a true "riddle" in every sense.

City of Angels

'City of Angels' really is one of Kershaw's most musically adventurous pieces. It feels like the sound of a songwriter and arranger pushing against the edges of what 1980s pop could be – a song that's clever, challenging, but also deeply rewarding once its unusual rhythms and melodies begin to make sense.

From its very first moments, 'City of Angels' declares itself as something offbeat. The opening bars sway in

3/4 time, instantly giving the piece a waltz-like feel. The synth melody lilts gracefully over the rhythm, whimsical and slightly surreal – something that wouldn't sound out of place in a dream sequence. It's disarming and delicate, far removed from the usual pulse of mid-eighties pop.

Then, just when the listener has adjusted to that gentle triple-time sway, Kershaw flips the rug. The verse enters – suddenly funky, syncopated, and ambiguous in its pulse. The bass and drums shift the ground beneath your feet; the time signature seems to blur into something far looser, somewhere around swing and shuffle. It's a transformation that catches you off guard, making the return of the 3/4 motif later all the more surprising.

The verses and choruses refuse to sit comfortably in any one rhythmic feel. The groove teases at a shuffle – that triplet swing that makes everything lean slightly forward – but Kershaw complicates it with syncopated bass figures and offbeat accents. It's music that's alive with movement, as if the song is constantly turning corners. That rhythmic slipperiness mirrors the song's lyrical setting – likely Los Angeles, a city of illusions and surfaces, where nothing is quite what it seems.

When Kershaw sings "Talk to the doctor. He turns acid into wine," the walking bass line suddenly evokes the blues, grounding the moment in something earthy and familiar. It's the same when he hits "Don't mess with me 'cos I've a bigger house than you" – that same blues-walk returns, sly and ironic, underpinning the satire in his vocal delivery. These tiny stylistic shifts – jazz, blues, funk, waltz – make 'City of Angels' feel like a miniature musical theatre piece disguised as a pop song.

The chorus, with its ascending melodic lines and clever harmonic turns, opens the space up beautifully. Kershaw's voice soars with conviction, and yet there's a touch of cynicism under the smooth melody. The irony is palpable – a commentary on image, fame, and the delusion of self-belief that fuels the world he's describing.

Later in the piece, as the chorus returns, melodic figures that echo the song's 3/4 introduction are weaved in – but now reimagined within the funkier, syncopated rhythm. It's a clever compositional move: the whimsical motif from the beginning doesn't just reappear; it's absorbed and reshaped into the fabric of the song's groove. The result feels cohesive yet surprising – a musical puzzle in sound.

The guitar solo is striking. It's not flashy, but gorgeously phrased – warm tone, lyrical bends, and perfect placement. Around it, the rhythm section plays these stop-start patterns that command attention: tiny moments of silence, sudden jolts, sharp accents. The effect is dramatic and slightly theatrical, forcing you to listen actively rather than drift along passively.

What's most impressive about 'City of Angels' is in how its complexity never feels pretentious or alienating. Instead, each strange rhythm or harmonic twist pulls you in deeper. It's the kind of song that unfolds over repeated listens, revealing new corners each time – a hallmark of sophisticated songwriting.

By the time the piece ends, you're left marvelling at its audacity. It's a track that could have been a disaster in lesser hands – too jazzy, too structurally odd – but Kershaw makes it coherent through sheer melodic intelligence and rhythmic flair. It stands as proof that he wasn't merely a pop craftsman but a true musical thinker.

In the context of *The Riddle*, 'City of Angels' acts as a manifesto of sorts: playful, daring, full of stylistic detours. It's music for listeners who like to be challenged – pop for the curious and attentive. Far from being background music, it insists on engagement.

Roses

'Roses' is a fascinating track in *The Riddle*'s lineup, and one that showcases Kershaw's flair for blending musical ingenuity with biting social commentary. It's intricate, thematically darkly humorous, and rhythmically irresistible – another example of his ability to wrap sharp intelligence in an accessible pop form.

'Roses' opens not with melody but with rhythm – an insistent percussion-led introduction that immediately draws attention to texture and movement rather than harmony. The first moments are filled with metallic-sounding percussive timbres that lend a world music flavour, rich in syncopation and colour. It's a groove that feels organic and tactile, giving the illusion of melody even before any pitched instrument enters.

This percussion motif carries the listener through the first few lyrical lines – from "Make it plastic, make it pay" through to "more or less." During this passage, Kershaw's vocal rhythm locks tightly with the percussion, making the words themselves almost percussive. There's a hypnotic, chant-like quality here, one that sets up a tone of sardonic detachment – a man observing the madness of modern, disposable society through a cynical lens.

The sonic world changes subtly but decisively with the line "Burn our time down to size." At this point, a synth sound enters to quietly assume melodic duties. The texture opens out, with airy, resonant tones tracing a loose melodic line over the continuing percussion bed. It's a transition that feels both inevitable and surprising.

By the time Kershaw reaches "just come from a meeting," the arrangement deepens. The bass arrives, rich and rubbery, adding a strong syncopated pulse that brings the track's groove fully into focus. The bass line now provides the backbone, underpinning Kershaw's satire of bureaucratic complacency. The bass line is central to the song's character – playful and constantly ducking and weaving around the beat. Its rhythm almost mimics sarcasm, poking fun at the lyrics it underlines. In the lines "we've just come from a meeting, and we're sure you'd like to know" and "we've talked to the experts and they know a thing or two," it seems to punctuate the irony of corporate reassurance with clever rhythmic nudges. This interplay between words and rhythm gives 'Roses' a sly, knowing intelligence that elevates it far beyond straightforward synth-pop.

The chorus is where 'Roses' reveals its true sting. The

line "And everything's coming up roses, or so they tell you" is delivered with an eerie cheerfulness, undercut by distorted vocal effects and a slightly off-kilter harmonic palette. These warped voices and doubled effects give the illusion of voices crowding around you – a sonic embodiment of collective delusion, as if propaganda were being broadcast from within the mix itself. There's a faint echo of paranoia in the production, the optimism of the phrase "coming up roses" hollowed out by the uneasy soundscape.

The track takes another intriguing turn with the passage beginning "But it's an awful price we pay." Here, a new texture is introduced – the percussion loosens, the synth pads widen, and a subtly different melodic contour takes hold. The harmony shifts into more ambiguous territory, the rhythm relaxing into a slightly freer pulse. It feels like the moment where the song finally exhales after so much tight, cynical precision. There's a brief sense of melancholy introspection before the "brown, brown grass..." part begins, where the rhythmic insistence and sardonic tone reassert themselves. It's a moment of clarity – almost empathy – before the cynicism returns, making the song's social bite even sharper.

Towards the end of the song, a guitar solo cuts through the mix. It plays the first two notes that would have formed the syllables of "roses" had Kershaw sung them after the line "everything's coming up." It's a musically surprising touch – an instrumental voice stepping in mid-thought, completing the phrase without words. The effect is immediate and attention-grabbing: a flash of melodic wit that blurs the line between lyric and arrangement. The solo is short and melodic rather than indulgent – perfectly phrased, like a quick flash of emotion. The guitar then weaves through the closing chorus, at times responding to the vocals – echoing both the melody and rhythm of the word "roses."

'Roses' is a sophisticated piece – a track that fuses world-music-inspired percussion, funk-inflected bass, sardonic pop melody, and a hint of experimental sound design. Lyrically, it's pure cynicism wrapped in sweetness – a critique of complacency dressed as reassurance.

'Roses' demonstrates how deftly Kershaw could balance accessibility and intellect. Beneath the catchy rhythm and sleek eighties production lies a genuinely sharp mind at work – one aware of the contradictions between optimism and apathy, melody and meaning, humanity and machinery.

Wide Boy

From its very first moments, 'Wide Boy' announces itself as the work of an artist who understands how to make pop music feel alive. Following the initial guitar and synth texture, the introductory synth hook immediately sets a mood that is both bright and faintly wistful. It's a melody that catches the ear straight away – clean, simple, and beautifully phrased – yet it carries a subtle sense of poignancy, as though there's something bittersweet hiding beneath its surface sheen. That tension, between cheerfulness and quiet melancholy, is part of what makes 'Wide Boy' such a satisfying listen.

Once the verse begins, the groove settles into a smooth, mid-tempo pop rhythm that feels natural and easy, driven by a steady drum pulse and buoyant bass line. The chords move with a kind of logic that feels inevitable once you've heard it – a hallmark of good songwriting. You can sense Kershaw's attention to structure here: every verse leads effortlessly into the chorus, each melodic line perfectly shaped to set up the next.

The chorus is one of Kershaw's most instantly memorable. The refrain – "He no big deal, he just a wide boy" – is delivered with a light touch, equal parts affectionate and ironic. Across the chorus, the melody soars upward before curling neatly back down again, creating a circular motion that mirrors the song's theme: a character trapped in a loop of image and fame. It's infectious and easy to follow, yet there's sophistication in the phrasing – the way the stresses fall slightly off the beat, giving it a subtle swing that keeps the listener's ear engaged.

Instrumentally, 'Wide Boy' is full of small but telling details. The synth textures are gleaming and smooth, typical of eighties pop but arranged here with particular care – layers that shimmer without cluttering the sound. The rhythm guitar adds punctuation throughout the verses, its clean, percussive tone giving the track extra drive. The bass moves fluidly beneath it all, providing motion and warmth while locking in tightly with the drum groove.

The guitar solo that arrives following the initial chorus is a perfect fit: bright, playful, and melodically clear.

Rather than being showy, it's a solo that feels like part of the storytelling. There's an optimism in its tone, the phrasing matching the upbeat personality of the track. It lifts the mood even higher, reminding the listener that while the lyrics poke fun at superficial stardom, the music itself is pure joy. In fact, there's even something of a folk-inspired melody going on in that solo – another instance of Kershaw's ability to make perfectly palatable pop that carries broader influences with ease.

Part of the song's quiet brilliance is that it manages to be both satire and celebration. The lyrics sketch the portrait of a pop star who has "no sense but he got money," a "wide boy" who's achieved overnight fame through charm and bravado rather than substance. Yet the music refuses to sneer – instead, it dances. There's an empathy to the way Kershaw delivers the lines, more amused observation than judgement. The contrast between the smooth, easy melody and the critical undercurrent in the words gives 'Wide Boy' its charm.

Rhythmically, there's more going on than meets the ear. Kershaw plays with syncopation subtly – the vocal phrasing often lands just before or just after the main beat, lending a conversational quality to the delivery. The result is music that feels spontaneous and natural, even though every detail is meticulously crafted. That balance – between precision and looseness, intellect and instinct – is what separates Kershaw from many of his contemporaries.

In the context of *The Riddle*, 'Wide Boy' feels like a moment of ease after the textural complexities of 'Roses' and the shifting time signatures of 'City of

Angels.' It's also a clear single contender – and indeed, its release as such made perfect sense. This is Kershaw at his most inviting, his knack for melodic architecture on full display, yet still infused with the intelligence and subtle emotion that make his music endure.

There's a generosity in 'Wide Boy.' It's music that welcomes the listener in, stays in your head, and rewards repeat listens. Its hooks shine brightly, its rhythm bounces with good humour, and through it all, Kershaw's voice carries that unmistakable blend of warmth and wit.

Save the Whale

After the rhythmic variety and melodic sparkle of *The Riddle*'s preceding tracks, 'Save the Whale' feels like stepping into another world entirely – a vast, hushed seascape where time slows and emotion deepens. The song's spacious texture announces itself immediately. Its opening bars are almost minimalist: soft synth pads shimmer like distant water, and a restrained pulse holds everything in suspension. Even when the verse begins, little else is added to fill the space. The arrangement breathes, each sound providing emotional resonance rather than density.

This restraint makes 'Save the Whale' haunting from the start. The harmonic language hovers delicately between major and minor, never settling fully into either – as though mirroring the uneasy co-existence between beauty and tragedy. These subtle tonal shifts give the song an emotional ambiguity that's both mournful and strangely soothing. It's not a protest anthem, but rather an elegy; sorrow seen through compassion rather than explicit outrage.

The lyric "You should never trust man, my friends" captures the song's devastating irony. Kershaw adopts the perspective of a human addressing whales, yet the tone is confessional, almost apologetic – as if he's warning them about his own species. In the early 1980s, the anti-whaling movement was gaining real public visibility, with campaigns from Greenpeace and others appearing regularly in the news. Kershaw seems to have absorbed that cultural moment and transformed it into something deeply personal. His song doesn't shout its message; it sighs it.

Towards the end of the first chorus, a haunting piano motif enters – sparse, echoing, and achingly simple. Its descending notes fall like tears, and from this point onward, the piano becomes a focal point in the song's texture. When the second verse begins, the piano remains, adding new weight and richness. It's as if the song has found its emotional vocabulary and now begins to elaborate upon it, layer by layer.

There's a moment of particular poignancy when Kershaw sings, "The giant dies trusting in me." The guilt embedded in that line is amplified by what follows: a synth solo that weaves gently above the continuing piano melody. The solo doesn't blaze or dominate – instead, it seems to mourn, its phrases curling around the chords like echoes of whale song itself. It's a beautiful instrumental moment: fragile, melodic, and filled with empathy.

When the lyric "Any other world would scream enough" occurs towards the end of the song, Kershaw gives the line a kind of quiet finality – not an accusation, but an admission of failure. Humanity, he implies, has the capacity to see the cruelty of its actions but somehow stops short of change. The music mirrors that sense of resignation: still graceful, but tinged with sorrowful inevitability.

Towards the end, another synth voice enters, broadening the texture. The layers begin to shimmer together – not in crescendo, but in a kind of widening emotional panorama. It feels like the ocean itself speaking back, immense and mournful.

The slow pace of the piece is crucial to its impact. After the rhythmic and harmonic diversity of the album, after the funk, the samba, the folk, the complex pop structures, 'Save the Whale' closes the record in stillness. It feels meditative, reflective, even cleansing, like a deep breath after the whirlwind of ideas that came before. As the final track, it's a perfect choice: gentle yet morally charged, a quiet statement about responsibility and empathy that lingers long after the music fades.

For all its serious subject matter, there's a strangely mellow quality to the song. The gentle major inflections offer warmth, a faint glimmer of hope, while the minor turns introduce unease, as though reminding us that beauty can exist even in mourning. The result is emotionally complex but not heavy-handed. It feels sincere, human, and movingly humble.

'Save the Whale' may not have been a single, but as a piece of songwriting it encapsulates what made Kershaw such an unusual pop figure of the 1980s: a musician unafraid to mix intellect with feeling, to bring moral weight into melodic form, and to close an album not with a bang, but with a whisper that echoes after the sound has gone.

Beyond the Breakthrough Period: The Later Eighties Albums

Kershaw's creative momentum didn't stop with *The Riddle*. Two more albums would follow in the eighties. *Radio Musicola*, released in October 1986, arrived nearly two years after *The Riddle* – an eternity in pop years. Musically, it was just as enchanting as anything Kershaw had done before. The title track alone justified the album's existence: a bass-driven soundscape with infectious rhythms and ideas that demand repeated listening. This was sophisticated pop that refused to talk down to its audience.

Yet commercially, the album struggled. Peaking at number forty-seven in the UK, it marked the beginning of what industry observers would call a downturn. Four singles emerged – 'When a Heart Beats,' 'Nobody Knows,' 'Radio Musicola,' and 'James Cagney' – but none breached the top twenty.

Kershaw has since reflected that timing was against him. The long gap after *The Riddle* meant public appetite had cooled, and the musical landscape had shifted – not necessarily tremendously, but enough for it to be impactful. By late 1986, the pop world was moving towards different sounds – Stock, Aitken and

Waterman were ascending, house music was emerging. *Radio Musicola* might have been excellent, but to an extent, it was swimming against the current.

With hindsight, the album's commercial performance feels irrelevant. The music exists, brilliant and enduring, long after chart positions have ceased to matter. Besides, when your first two albums have set the bar at platinum-selling, chart-topping heights, anything less could feel like failure even when it isn't. *Radio Musicola* was certified silver – still a significant achievement that most artists would celebrate.

The Works followed in May 1989, and if *Radio Musicola* had struggled, this one barely registered commercially. 'One Step Ahead' limped to number fifty-five; 'Elisabeth's Eyes' didn't chart at all. The industry had moved on, apparently.

But listen to these songs – really listen – and the commercial lack of recognition becomes incomprehensible. 'One Step Ahead' contains melodic passages as beautiful as anything on *Human Racing* or *The Riddle*. The melody that carries "I work all day and I think all night..." embodies the same kind of yearning complexity found in 'Wouldn't It Be Good,' while the bass line grooves with characteristic Kershaw brilliance.

'Elisabeth's Eyes' represents something even more profound: Kershaw at his most socially conscious and emotionally sophisticated. Inspired by the correspondence between Elisabeth Allan (an Essex teacher) and Willie Darden (who spent fourteen years on Florida's death row before execution in 1988), the song emerged from Kershaw reading about Allan's campaign just days before Darden died.

"For reasons she didn't really understand, Elisabeth began to write to him in prison and he wrote back," Kershaw explained to Simon Mayo in 1989. "Towards the end he was writing three or four times a day. They never met, but she was his one link with the outside world." After researching Darden's case, Kershaw became convinced of his innocence. As he told the *Sunday Mercury*, "Death row wasn't something that concerned me before... Any new subject you start finding out about changes your life."

The resulting song manages something extraordinary: addressing capital punishment and miscarriage of justice while remaining musically uplifting. Opening with an almost dreamlike guitar passage, settling into a subtle reggae-influenced rhythm, building to that steady, hopeful chorus – "My hope lies in Elisabeth's eyes..." – it's masterful songwriting that transcends its dark subject matter.

The depth of Kershaw's commitment to 'Elisabeth's Eyes' reveals itself in how thoroughly he immersed himself in the story. During a BBC *Going Live!* broadcast in April 1989, filmed in Berlin where he was supporting Elton John on tour, Kershaw revealed he had studied the actual correspondence between Allan and Darden. "I've read some of the letters, which are absolutely unbelievable – they're poetry, they're love letters, they're incredible." This wasn't a songwriter mining tragedy for material; this was an artist genuinely moved by a human story, determined to do it justice.

While 'The Riddle' may have cemented Kershaw's reputation as someone who prioritised sound over sense, his broader catalogue reveals a sophisticated storyteller working through multiple perspectives and narrative devices. 'Elisabeth's Eyes' demonstrates this perfectly – the opening verse begins with "*I* told my tale with some words," placing us firmly in Darden's voice, seeing through his eyes, feeling his desperate hope. This isn't just sympathetic observation; it's complete inhabitation of character.

This narrative sophistication appears throughout Kershaw's work. 'I Won't Let the Sun Go Down on Me' shifts perspective brilliantly, with the first verse sung from the politician's viewpoint – "Forty winks in the lobby, make *mine* a G and T, then to *our* favourite hobby" – the pronouns revealing we're inside the mind of power, not observing it. 'Wouldn't It Be Good' takes yet another approach, with each verse representing a different speaker in conversation: "*I* got it bad," each one claims, before being answered by the next voice in the chain of universal complaint.

Sometimes Kershaw positions himself as external narrator, creating miniature character studies. In 'Dancing Girls,' we're told "Our hero sits with head in hands" – we're watching someone watching someone else, layers of observation that create emotional distance and intimacy simultaneously. 'Don Quixote' addresses its subject directly – "Don Quixote, what do you say?" – turning the listener into interrogator of this reimagined literary figure.

These aren't just clever lyrical tricks; they're evidence

of a songwriter who understood that pop songs could be vehicles for complex storytelling. Whether channelling death row prisoners, corrupt politicians, or shouting-at-windmills dreamers, Kershaw proved that pop songs could contain entire worlds, multiple voices, and profound empathy. The fact that he could do this while also crafting irresistible melodies – that's the real magic.

That 'Elisabeth's Eyes' found no commercial home in 1989 says nothing about the song and everything about the arbitrary nature of pop success. This was Kershaw operating at peak artistic power, crafting something profound and beautiful that happened to arrive when the world was looking elsewhere.

These later eighties albums deserve recognition not as commercial failures but as artistic triumphs. Yes, the 1984 albums were phenomenal, capturing lightning in a very particular bottle. But to stop there, to ignore *Radio Musicola* and *The Works*, would be to miss crucial chapters in Kershaw's catalogue.

The music industry might have moved on by 1986, but the music itself remains. For anyone genuinely interested in Kershaw's artistry rather than his chart positions, these albums offer rewards equal to their more celebrated predecessors. They're reminders that commercial success and artistic worth are often entirely different measurements, and that sometimes excellent music lands when nobody's paying attention.

The Long Game:
Beyond 1984 and Back Again

There's a particular challenge that faces artists whose early work burned so brightly it threatens to eclipse everything that follows. The temptation to resist that gravitational pull is understandable – no artist wants to become a parody of themselves, endlessly mining the same seam until it's exhausted. Kershaw has been refreshingly honest about his initial reluctance to embrace the nostalgia circuit, wary of being known only as the man with the snood and the mysterious riddle ("There is nothing about the eighties that I want to revive," he once said in 1999). Yet he's also acknowledged the unexpected rewards of accepting what those songs mean to people, and the genuine pleasure of sharing stages with contemporaries who rode the same eighties wave.

The relationship between artist and artwork becomes increasingly complex over time. While fans carry these songs as personal soundtracks through decades of their lives, the artist moves forward, creates new work, lives beyond that captured moment. This disconnect was brilliantly illustrated during Kershaw's 1999 appearance on *Never Mind the Buzzcocks*. When Mark Lamarr asked for the lyrics that follow on from "Don Quixote, what do you say?" Kershaw stumbled over his own words before quipping, "I sing it every bloody night!" One imagines fans across Britain shouting the correct lyrics at their televisions – knowing the songs better than their creator, preserving them more faithfully in memory than the man who wrote them. It's a perfect encapsulation of how art can mean just as much to its audience as its author. (To be fair to Kershaw, though, this was quickfire comedy panel show territory, complete with all the amusing distractions and rapid-pace banter that format demands – hardly the ideal environment for perfect recall of lyrics written fifteen years earlier.)

To see Kershaw only through the lens of 1984 is to miss the breadth of a career that spans over four decades. His songwriter's craft found new outlets, most famously with 'The One and Only,' written in 1989 and then featured in the 1991 film *Buddy's Song*. The track became a UK number one for the film's star, Chesney Hawkes, achieving that rare status of genuinely ubiquitous hit – the song everyone knows even if they can't name its writer. Its endurance is proven by Hawkes performing a new version (mixed by Sigala) for Waitrose's 2025 Christmas advertisement, introducing Kershaw's songwriting to yet another generation who might not even have been born when the original topped the charts.

The collaborative side of Kershaw's career reads like a who's who of popular music. Working with Elton John, Bonnie Tyler, and Sia represents just the tip of an impressive iceberg. To catalogue every collaboration, every writing credit, every behind-the-scenes contribution would require another book entirely. Each represents another facet of a career that refused to be defined by two albums, however brilliant they are.

In 2024, Kershaw embarked on The 1984 Tour, performing both *Human Racing* and *The Riddle* in their entirety. This wasn't reluctant nostalgia or cynical cash-grabbing – it was recognition, celebration, and reciprocation. Now, over forty years on, these albums still deserve to be heard complete, in sequence, as cohesive statements. The tour acknowledged what fans have long known: these weren't just collections of singles plus other songs, but complete artistic visions that reward full immersion. That audiences still fill venues to hear these songs speaks to their enduring power – they haven't become relics, but remain living, breathing music.

Finale: The Enduring Magic

As we close this celebration of Nik Kershaw's artistry, what emerges is something increasingly rare in popular music: genuine craft that transcends its commercial moment. From an unemployment benefit office in Suffolk to the stages of the world, from experimental beginnings with Fusion to collaborations with music royalty, this has been a career built on substance rather than style – even if the style was pretty memorable too.

The songs we've explored here – with their hidden complexities, their sophisticated harmonies masquerading as simple pop, their nonsense lyrics that somehow made perfect sense – remain as vital today as they were over four decades ago. They've soundtracked first loves and break-ups, car journeys and wedding dances, nostalgic nights and brand new discoveries. Each generation finds something different in them, yet they never lose their essential magic.

Perhaps the greatest testament to Kershaw's achievement is that these songs don't require nostalgia to work. Yes, for those who were there, they're time machines back to 1984. But play 'Wouldn't It Be Good' to someone who's never heard it, and watch their face light up at that chorus. Play 'The Riddle' and see them puzzle over lyrics that mean nothing and everything simultaneously.

Kershaw continues to write, to perform, to create. The riddle of his enduring appeal isn't really a riddle at all – it's what happens when genuine musical intelligence meets pop sensibility, when craft serves emotion, when complexity dances with accessibility.

In an industry that often mistakes novelty for innovation and volume for value, Nik Kershaw's career stands as a reminder of what popular music can achieve when it's created with care, intelligence, and respect for the audience. The human race needs music like this – music that works on multiple levels, that rewards repeated listening, that treats pop as an art form worthy of serious attention while never forgetting to be joyful.

Our analysis confirms what millions of listeners already knew: great songwriting transcends its moment. Kershaw's music proved it then, and it's still proving it now.

www.ingramcontent.com/pod-product-compliance
Lightning Source LLC
Chambersburg PA
CBHW030326080526
44584CB00012B/733